The Hiker's Guide
to NEVADA

By Bruce Grubbs

FALCON PRESS®

Recreation Guides from Falcon Press

The Angler's Guide to Montana
The Hiker's Guide to Colorado
The Beartooth Fishing Guide
The Hiker's Guide to Idaho
The Floater's Guide to Colorado
The Hiker's Guide to Utah
The Hiker's Guide to New Mexico
The Hiker's Guide to Arizona
The Hiker's Guide to Washington
The Hiker's Guide to California
The Hunter's Guide to Montana
The Rockhound's Guide to Montana
The Hiker's Guide to Montana's Continental Divide Trail
The Hiker's Guide to Hot Springs in the Pacific Northwest
Recreation Guide to California's National Forests

Falcon Press is continually expanding its list of recreational guidebooks using the same general format as this book. All books include detailed descriptions, accurate maps, and all information necessary for enjoyable trips. You can order extra copies of this book and get information and prices for the books listed above by writing Falcon Press, P.O. Box 1718, Helena, MT 59624. Also, please ask for a free copy of our current catalog listing all Falcon Press books.

Library of Congress Catalog Card Number: 91-070768
ISBN: 1-56044-063-5

Manufactured in the United States of America.

Falcon Press Publishing Co., Inc.
P.O. Box 1718, Helena, MT 59624

All text and maps, by the author.
Photos by the author except as noted.
Cover Photo: by Mark Muench, Wheeler Peak.

ACKNOWLEDGMENTS

I wish to thank my friends and hiking companions over the years who suggested new areas to hike and often accompanied me in the backcountry. Specifically, I wish to thank the personnel of the Bureau of Land Management, the US Fish and Wildlife Service, the US Forest Service, and the National Park Service for their valuable contributions, as well as Ron Kezar for his contribution. Thank you to Marjorie Sill, who wrote the afterword, "Nevada's Wilderness Challenge". The book would not have been possible without their help.

Thanks go to Duart Martin for invaluable proofreading and editing, and to Stewart Aitchison for suggesting the project and providing assistance along the way. And finally, I wish to thank all the fine folks at Falcon Press who made this guide a reality.—*Bruce Grubbs*

CONTENTS

INTRODUCTION

HIKING TECHNIQUES & ETHICS

MAKING IT A SAFE TRIP

THE HIKES

AFTERWORD

A HIKERS BASIC CHECKLIST

RESOURCES

FURTHER READING

FINDING MAPS

ABOUT THE AUTHOR

PREFACE

Nevada, the Silver State, is associated more with mining and gambling than hiking in many people's minds. But most of Nevada is the rugged backcountry where the rich contrast between valley and mountain is most apparent to the foot explorer. Nevada has desert salt flats shimmering in the sun and cool mountain streams cascading down rocky slopes, shady redrock canyons and dramatic alpine peaks, aspen and the ancient bristlecone pines.

A Nevada hike can vary from an easy stroll on an interpretive nature trail to a strenuous multiday backpack trip. Hikes of both extremes as well as intermediate walks are represented here. This book is an invitation to escape from the man-made world and discover a world where nature still dominates and time runs on a far slower scale.

MAP OF NEVADA

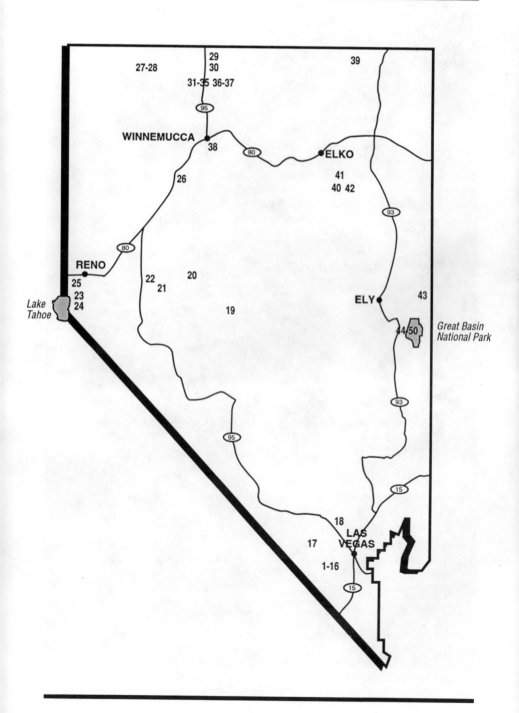

Nevada hikers have a surprising abundance of backcountry possibilities from which to choose. Here a hiker climbs above timberline on Toiyabe Summit Trail.

INTRODUCTION

Hiking in Nevada

This book is a sampling of the hiking and backpacking available in Nevada. An attempt has been made to include the widest possible variety of hiking, not only to benefit you, the reader, but also to publicize areas of the state in which hiking is threatened by non-compatible uses. Little-known and less traveled hikes are represented, as well as more popular areas. Information on interesting natural history of the area is included with most of the hike descriptions. Use this book as a starting point for your own explorations of this varied region of the Southwest.

Geology and Geography

Most of Nevada lies within the portion of the American West known as the Great Basin; an area that includes parts of California, Oregon, Idaho, and Utah. Within the Great Basin, all of the mountain drainage flows into closed valleys, or basins, and no water reaches the sea. More than 160 parallel mountain ranges, all trending north-south, drain into some ninety valleys, The majority of these isolated mountains are in Nevada. While a few valleys contain lakes, most feature salt flats where the infrequent stream flows from the mountains evaporate, leaving behind a crust of white minerals.

Within Nevada, the elevation ranges from 300 feet above sea level to a high of over 13,000. The average elevation is approximately 5,500 feet. The lowest valleys and mountains are generally in the southern and western part of the state, with elevations increasing toward the north and east. Boundary Peak, highest in the state at 13,145 feet, is the northernmost peak of the 14,000 foot White Mountains which lie mostly in California. The Snake Range is the most lofty in the state, culminating in the glacier- carved summit of Wheeler Peak.

Millions of years ago during the formation of the North American continent, the area that is now Nevada was stretched from east to west by crustal forces. Numerous north-tending fractures, or faults, formed as the rocks broke under the strain. Some of the resulting blocks sank to form the valleys, while others rose to form the mountains. As the faulting continues to lower the basins and raise the mountains, erosion from water flowing downhill tends to wear down the mountains and fill the valleys. The topography we see today reflects the fact that the faulting is still active enough to keep the mountains from being worn down to a flat plain.

More recently, as these events go, a colder and wetter climate caused snow to accumulate in the higher ranges and form glaciers. The last of these ice ages ended about 10,000 years ago but left their mark on the topography in the form of steep, glacially carved mountain peaks and classic U-shaped mountain valleys. As the climate warmed and the glaciers receded, the massive flow of meltwater collected in huge lakes rivaling the Great Lakes in size. In many parts of Nevada, the ancient shorelines of these lakes are clearly visible as terraces along the lower mountain slopes.

During the cooler glacial climate, extensive forests covered the valleys and bordered the lakes. As the last ice age gradually ended, the warming climate

Wheeler Peak, at 13,063 feet is Nevada's highest mountain but not its highest point. That honor goes to Boundary Peak, a northern outlier of the White Mountains which lie mostly in California. A good trail leads to the summit but caution must be used whenever snow covers the higher slopes. Stewart Aitchison

caused plants and animals which had adapted to a cooler, wetter climate to migrate up the mountainsides.

Natural History

Most wet weather reaches Nevada from the west and northwest, in the form of Pacific storms. Much of the moisture from these winter storms falls on the high Sierra Nevada and the Cascade Mountains before reaching Nevada. The moisture that is left tends to fall on the mountains rather than the valleys. Precipitation varies from five inches in the driest valleys to eighteen inches in the higher eastern Nevada ranges. Temperatures range from thirty or forty below zero Fahrenheit up to 115 degrees. Most of the precipitation falls as snow. Much of Nevada is too hot for enjoyable hiking in the summer, and some of it is too cold in the winter. The best hiking seasons are spring and fall, but because of the great elevation range the higher mountains are best in summer, and the lower deserts are best enjoyed in winter.

This great variation of climate within the state makes life interesting for the native plants and animals as well. Most plants and many animals are adapted to a limited range of temperature and moisture, and so different communities are found at various elevations in the valleys and mountains. Valleys in central and western Nevada feature tough desert shrubs; shadscale, bud sage, greasewood and salt bush. Lower valleys in southern Nevada are covered with creosote bush, mesquite and the striking Joshua tree, while the higher valleys are dominated by sage brush. This shrub-grassland covers nine-tenths of the state. The most common animal is the rabbit, but coyotes, gophers, the red fox and the western badger may also be found. Antelope and wild horses favor the open valleys, while mule deer range from desert to mountain depending on the season. Generally the reptiles prefer the deserts—these include rattlesnakes as well as harmless snakes and numerous varieties of lizards.

Throughout the state, mountain streams are bordered by aspen, alder, chokecherry, cottonwood, water birch and willow. These locations are favored by beaver as well as many bird species. Rainbow trout has been introduced to many streams throughout the state.

Surprisingly, waterfowl are common along the desert lakes and marshes, and the rarity of desert water makes this habitat all the more precious.

Human History

It appears that the first humans arrived in Nevada between 13,000 and 10,000 years ago, probably as a result of migrations from Siberia via the Bering Strait toward the end of the last ice age. Numerous archaeological sites are helping to tell the story of early man in Nevada. (These sites are protected by Federal law, and if they are disturbed, another piece of the story is gone forever.) The timing of man's arrival coincided with the last of the great glacial lakes. These early people took advantage of the easy living provided by the lakes, catching fish as well as hunting the native American horse and camel. Others appeared to specialize in hunting mammoths. Most lived in caves or crude shelters, but toward the end of the prehistoric period, around 1000 AD, a Pueblo culture of well-organized communities developed. Some of these sites contained well over 100 houses.

After about 1100 AD the more advanced communities were abandoned, for unknown reasons. Some of the people may have migrated elsewhere, and some

When a large glacier erodes deep canyons and sharp Matterhorn-like peaks, it does so by grinding down deeply near the heads of the canyons where the snow accumulates, and also pushes masses of rock debris ahead of the ice to form natural dams. Later, when the ice melts, these depressions are filled by crystal clear melt water, forming beautiful alpine lakes.

probably became the ancestors of the tribes discovered by Europeans.

Four major Native American groups occupied Nevada, with the Southern Paiutes probably being the first tribe encountered by Europeans at the southern end of the state. The Northern Paiutes occupied the western third of Nevada, and the Western Shoshones roamed the eastern half. A smaller group, the Washoes, ranged along the eastern Sierra Nevada.

By the time the white man arrived, the Nevada climate made it difficult for the natives to wrest a living from the land. Most of the Native Americans were hunter-gatherers, migrating constantly to take advantage of the seasons. Recreation time was mostly limited to harvest gatherings or communal hunts.

Probably the first European to enter Nevada was Father Francisco Garces, part of a larger Spanish expedition seeking a more direct route from Santa Fe to Monterrey in 1776. Competition between British and American fur trappers heated up in 1826, when Jedediah Smith led an expedition across the southern tip of Nevada to California, then crossed the central part of the state from west to east. Another trapper, Peter S. Ogden, entered northern Nevada in 1828 and worked his way south and east to Utah. Further explorations by Ogden opened up the route along the Humboldt River across the northern third of Nevada, a route later used by wagon trains of emigrants headed for the Pacific Coast.

The earliest emigrants were trespassing on Mexican soil, but by 1850 Nevada was part of the American Territory of Utah. Discovery of gold in California caused the tiny trickle of emigrants to become a flood. Most of the parties used the Humboldt River route, still a major corridor of travel across Nevada.

Inevitably, trading posts sprang up along the emigrant trails, while others stayed behind to try their hand at ranching and mining. By 1860, when Nevada became a territory, significant deposits of gold and silver had been discovered in the Virginia City area—the Comstock Lode. This caused a rapid population growth, and Nevada became a state in 1864. In comparison, neighboring Arizona Territory did not become a state until 1912.

Although ranching has been a staple of Nevada life since the early settlers arrived, mining has been responsible for most of the economic activity until recently. Although the boom-and-bust economy of mining has made life difficult for some Nevada communities, many Nevadans still view mining as essential to the state's welfare.

Since 1945, gambling, retirement communities and tourism have tended to supplant mining as the major source of income, although a modern gold strike in northern Nevada challenges that trend. Increasingly, Americans see the undeveloped portions of Nevada as precious areas to be protected, not just exploited. Although preservation is definitely still a minority view in Nevada, the recent establishment of Great Basin National Park, Nevada's first, has won support.

Ruins such as this one in the Toiyabe Range are protected by the federal Antiquities Act, which is intended to preserve our archaeological heritage.

HIKING TECHNIQUES AND ETHICS

Leave nothing but footprints...

Although the Native Americans and the early explorers and settlers lived off the land out of necessity, the modern hiker and backpacker finds maximum freedom in being virtually independent of the land. Carrying food, shelter and warmth in a reasonably light pack, the walker needs only water and a level place to sleep. This lightweight camping style means a camp can be established or broken in a matter of minutes rather than hours, leaving little trace of the hiker's presence. The ability to "leave nothing but footprints" could hardly have come at a better time. The shrinking American wilderness is under increasing pressure as a steadily growing population discovers the joy and serenity to be found in the outdoors. In the last century, a small population of miners easily destroyed much of Nevada's mountain forests. Today those same mountains can provide recreation for a much larger population, if each person will care for the land. The basic principles are easy.

While walking, stay on established human or animal trails if available, and avoid cutting switchbacks. Members of a large party traveling cross-country should spread out rather than create a new trail by walking single-file. These practices minimize soil erosion. In the Great Basin, the soil is often protected by a crusty surface composed of lichen and moss, which effectively slows erosion but takes years to reform once disturbed.

Very few hikers will deliberately litter, and much of what we see along the trail is accidental. Individual hikers can put an end to the litter problem by packing out a bit of someone else's litter at the end of each hike.

Look for campsites which are "hard", such as sand, gravel, hard dirt. With the better sleeping pads, even solid rock slabs make comfortable campsites, and offer the additional freedom to move around camp barefoot. Soft camp-sites, such as meadow grass or pine needles, must be used with great care to avoid destroying the ground cover. Rather than constructing a level bed or tent site, look for a natural one. Avoid having to dig drainage ditches by choosing a slightly elevated site where rain water will run away from your shelter. In heavily used areas, use an existing campsite rather than starting a new one. One of the major reasons people avoid old campsites is the litter and campfire rings left by old-style "heavy" campers. If time and load permits, clean up a messy campsite and leave a pleasant surprise for the next party. Ashes can be buried, blackened rocks scattered, and trash packed out if packs are light.

Although many hikers enjoy the freedom and relaxation of cooking meals on a backpacker's stove, for others a campfire is an essential part of the experience. In some situations campfires should not be built, such as in heavily used areas or near timberline where wood is scarce, and where prohibited by regulation. During the summer the fire danger may be extreme, and no fire should be built on a windy, dry day. Most of the time, it is possible to be a responsible hiker and still have a campfire. Use an established campfire ring if available. Otherwise look for a site in gravel, sand, or bare soil. Then

Using modern lightweight equipment, it is possible to camp in comfort with almost no impact on the country. Good sleeping pads mean a good night's rest with no need to scar the fragile alpine tundra, and lightweight stoves eliminate the need to build campfires.

dig a shallow pit, heaping the dirt around the edges to form a wind and fire break. Do not use stones, which become permanently blackened. Collect dead wood from the ground or the lower parts of trees by breaking by hand. If you need an ax or a saw, either the wood is too large or too scarce. Keep your fire small, both to avoid using large amounts of wood and to keep the amount of ashes small. Most backpacker's trash is so light it can be easily carried out. However, paper can be burned to reduce bulk. Note that many paper packages are lined with aluminum foil which does not burn.

When ready to leave camp, make certain the fire is cold, by mixing in water or dirt and stirring until there is no obvious smoke or heat. Then check with your bare hand, cover the fire pit with the dirt piled around the edges, and scatter any remaining wood. After a short time, your fire site will again look natural.

If lightweight food is carried (modern supermarkets are full of convenient items which make ideal backpacking food) and carefully repacked to eliminate excess packaging, the trash resulting from even a week or more in the backcountry can easily be carried out. Avoid burying food, because animals will find it by smell shortly after you leave and scatter it around the campsite. Human food is not very good for most wildlife.

Wilderness sanitation is the most critical skill needed to keep the backcountry pristine. A walk in any popular recreation area will show that few people seem to know how to relieve themselves away from facilities. In some areas naturally occurring diseases such as Giardiasis are being aggravated by poor human sanitation. Fortunately the rules are simple. If facilities are available, use them. Their presence means that the human population of the area is too large for the natural disposal systems of the soil. In the backcountry, select a site at least a hundred yards from streams, lakes and springs, then dig a small "cathole" about six inches into the organic layer of the soil. Some people carry a small plastic trowel for this purpose. Avoid barren, sandy soil if possible. When finished, fill the hole, covering any toilet paper. Burning toilet paper is a good idea only in moist areas where there is no fire danger.

Our archaeological and historical heritage

In the backcountry, the hiker will encounter artifacts of various ages. Some of these structures, tools, and other artifacts date from before European discovery of the Americas. Others were built by early settlers and explorers. All are valuable links with our history and prehistory. Yet increasingly this evidence of early civilization is being lost to vandalism. Federal laws have been passed to protect such antiquities, but ultimately the responsibility must lie with those who encounter artifacts. Keep in mind that the relationships between artifacts in a site are often more important than the artifacts themselves. Petroglyphs and pictographs (rock drawings) have lasted thousands of years but are susceptible to damage from thoughtless people.

MAKING IT A SAFE TRIP

Wilderness is a safe place to be. Nature is indifferent to hikers, in the sense that there are no malevolent forces. On the other hand there are no beneficial forces either. Thus the hiker must be self reliant. For many people, this total dependence on self is frightening. However, once a hiker develops confidence in his or her techniques, abilities and equipment, then operating in the back-country becomes a welcome relief from the complex tangle of civilized living. Wilderness decisions are sometimes important but usually simple. While "out there", things that seemed important in civilization lose some of their urgency. In other words, we gain a sense of perspective.

Most wilderness accidents are caused by individuals or parties pushing too hard. Set reasonable goals, allowing for delays from weather, deteriorated trails, unexpectedly rough country, and dry springs. Be flexible enough to cut out part of a hike if it appears that your original plans are too ambitious.

A few plants are hazardous to the touch, such as poison ivy and stinging nettle. Spiny plants like cactus are easy to avoid. Never eat any plant, unless you know what you are doing. Many common plants, especially mushrooms, are deadly.

Animals will leave you alone unless molested or provoked. Do not ever feed wild animals, as they rapidly get used to the handouts and then will vigorously defend their new food source. Around camp, problems with rodents can be avoided by hanging your food from rocks or trees. Even the toughest pack can be chewed up by a determined mouse or squirrel who has all night in which to work. Heavily used campsites present the worst problems, but in Nevada there's not much reason to camp in heavily used areas! Rattlesnakes cause concern but can easily be avoided. They usually warn off intruders by rattling well before you reach striking range. Since rattlesnakes can strike no further than half their body length, avoid placing your hands and feet in areas you cannot see, and walk several feet away from rock overhangs and shady ledges. Snakes prefer surfaces at about eighty degrees Fahrenheit, so during hot weather they prefer the shade of bushes or overhangs, and in cool weather will be found sunning themselves on open ground.

Water

In the desert, water is the most important consideration in planning a hike. On day hikes, make certain you carry enough. In hot weather, as much as two gallons per person per day may be required. On desert backpack trips, the route and itinerary are planned around water sources. It is convenient but not always possible to be near a spring or stream for lunch stops and at camps. Collapsible water bags that will hold up to two gallons are available and should be carried in addition to reliable plastic water bottles. Collapsible containers make it possible to carry water for a dry lunch or even a dry camp. Dry campsites are often very pleasant on ridges and hill tops. However, plan to reach one reliable water source per day, unless the weather is cool and you are experienced in dry camping.

Springs and streams shown on maps are often unreliable. The newest USGS topographic maps show all drainages with the symbol for permanent streams, which can be misleading. The best way to determine the reliability of desert water sources is through experience in the area, either yours or a trusted friend. Allowance must be made for springs and streams that may be dry— do not depend on any single water source. Be aware of reliable water sources that are off your route. Known water sources are listed in each hike description; there may be more water sources, but I have attempted to err on the side of caution.

Very few backcountry water sources are safe to drink. The exceptins are isolated springs and direct snow melt. Contamination has resulted from wild and domestic animals as well as the increasing human populatin. Infections from contaminated water are uncomfortable and can be disabling. Giardiasis, a severe gastrointestinal infectin, has received more attention recently. However recent evidence indicates that humans have probably been blamed for more than our share of responsibility, as the cysts that cause Giardiasis are spread by all mammals. Nevertheless, there is no doubt that poor back-country sanitatin has contributed to the problem.

So unfortunately, the rule must be; purify all water sources unless very sure they are uncontaminated. (Water containing Giardia cysts or other disease agents may be sparkling clear and cold.) Iodine water purification tablets, available from outsoor shops, are very effective. (See *Medicine for Mountaineering* in Further Reading), states that one iodine tablet will kill most problem organisms in a quart of water, including Giardia cysts. Read and follow carefully the directions on the bottle. Note that the tgalets must be kept dry to retain their effectiveness.

Filters have become increasingly popular, especially with large parties. Most filters are heavier than iodine tablets, but produce equally save water at lower cost and with less iodine aftertaste.

Chlorine tablets are not reliable for purifying wilderness water due to the common presence of organic matter (bits of leaves, etc.) that are harmless but use up the purifying agent. Also, chlorine tablets rapidly lose effectiveness once the original bottle is opened.

Weather

Nevada has an intermountain climate. The dry clear air allows strong radiation cooling so that temperatures often drom fifty degrees Fahrenheit by sunrise. Even the hottest areas generally have cool nights. Temperatures drop about five degrees Fahrenheit for each thousand foot rise in elevation, so mountain tops are often much cooler than lower slopes.

As mentioned earlier, Nevada receives most of its precipitation as snow, generally during the winter months. However, snow may fall at any time of year on the higher mountains. Be prepared by bringing more warm clothing than it appears you will need. During the cooler months, consider synthetic garments made of polypropylene or polyester fibers. These fibers retain their indulating ability when wet better than any natureal fiber, including wool. Avoid continuous exposure to chilling weather, which may subtly lower body temperature and cause sudden collapse from hypothermia, a life-threatening condition. Cool winds, especially with rain, are the most dangerous because the heat loss is insidious. Hypothermia may be completely prevented by wearing enough clothing and wind protectin to avoid chilling, and by eating and drinking regularly to keep the body fueled.

Hikers should be prepared for snow on the higher peaks at any time of the year. Cliff Leight

Spring, summer and fall are generally dry, though summer thunderstorms may develop, especially in southern and eastern Nevada. Since much hiking is in the mountains, lightning can present a hazard. Less obvious are the hazards associated with sudden heavy rain-flash flooding and rapid temperature drops. Keep in mind that the mountains are eroded mostly during spring runoff and flash floods. Avoid camping in stream beds and dry washes.

In hot weather, water is vital. Ensure that you have a reliable supply and then drink enough to satisfy your thirst and then some. Remember if it gets too heavy in your pack you can always drink it. Your body will use it efficiently.

Protection from the heat and the sun is important. Most people find a lightweight sun hat vital for desert hiking. During hot weather, plan hikes in the higher mountains to escape the heat, or hike early in the day to avoid the afternoon heat. Summer backpack trips can be planned to take advantage of the long days by hiking from first light to midmorning, taking a long, shady lunch break, and then finishing the day's walk in early evening when it cools off. At dusk, keep an eye out for rattlesnakes, as they are active in the evening during hot weather.

Finding and Using Maps

Each hike in this book is accompanied by a sketch map showing the access roads and the specific trail or route mentioned in the hike description. These maps are intended as general guides. More detailed maps are referred to in the heading and description of each hike, and will be useful or even essential.

Topographic maps published by the U.S. Geological Survey are usually the best for hiking. These maps are published in sheets, or quadrangles covering relatively small areas. Topography is shown in detail by means of contour lines, as well as manmade features such as trails, roads, buildings, etc. This information is very accurate at the date of publication, shown on the lower right corner of each map. Unfortunately the sheer number of maps (several thousand to cover a western state) makes updating a slow process, so often trail and road information is outdated. Many outdoor shops and some engineering and blueprint shops carry USGS maps. They are also available directly from the Geological Survey (see Finding Maps).

Other useful maps are published by the U.S. Forest Service and the Bureau of Land Management. These maps cover a larger area and are updated more often, though the topography is not shown. They are best used in conjunction with topographic maps. These maps are usually available from the office listed under "For More Information" in each hike description, and from some outdoor shops, and from the regional or state offices of the land management agencies (see Finding Maps).

Classic Forest Service enameled metal trail signs dating from the thirties are still found along the Toiyabe Summit Trail.

MAP LEGEND

Interstate	00		Described Trail and Trailhead	⊙--→
U.S. Highway	00		Cross-Country Route	·······→
State or Other Principal Road	000			
Forest Road	0000		Peak & Elevation	9731
Paved Road			Pass or Saddle	
Dirt Road	======		River, Creek, Drainage	
Building	■		Meadow or Swamp	

NEVADA

N

0	0.5	1

Miles

Trail Location
Symbol and Map Scale

Springs	
Lakes	
Glacier	
Camp site	▲

THE HIKES

The hikes are rated for relative difficulty as easy, moderate, or difficult. An easy hike is one with little elevation change, covering short distances on a maintained trail. Nearly anyone should be able to do these hikes. Difficult hikes involve major elevation change, long distances and possibly cross country hiking. These hikes should be attempted only by experienced hikers who are well aware of their abilities. Moderate hikes fall in between these extremes.

Please be aware that the perceived difficulty of a hike varies with the individual hiker, the season and the amount of trail maintenance.

HIKE 1 *MOENKOPI TRAIL*

General description: An easy loop hike on an interpretive trail in the Red Rock Canyon National Conservation Area.
General location: Approximately fifteen miles west of Las Vegas.
Maps: La Madre Mtn 7.5-minute USGS, BLM brochure.
Difficulty: Easy.
Length: Two miles round-trip.
Elevation: 3,700 feet.
Special attractions: Triassic fossils and diverse desert plant communities.
Water: None.
Best season: Fall through spring.
For more information: Red Rock Canyon National Conservation Area, Bureau of Land Management, PO Box 26569, Las Vegas, NV 89126; (702) 363-1921.
Permit: None (day use only).
Finding the trailhead: From Las Vegas, drive west on Charleston Blvd. (NV 159) to reach the Red Rock Scenic Loop, approximately eleven miles from the intersection of Charleston and Rainbow Blvds. Turn right (north) on the Scenic Loop road, then left to the Bureau of Land Management Visitor Center. Here you can obtain general information on the Red Rock area and check on the road and trail conditions.

The hike: The Moenkopi Trail starts southwest of the visitor center near the weather station. Along the way, watch for creosote, blackbrush and yucca-typical members of this desert plant community. The trail leads to the crest of the hill west of the visitor center. At the crest, cottontop barrel cactus and Triassic fossils can be seen.

Creosote bush, found along this trail and common in southern Nevada and the rest of the Mohave Desert, is an outstanding example of the extreme methods desert plants use to survive drought. During dry periods, the bush sheds its mature leaves as well as whole twigs and branches, retaining only

HIKES 1, 2, 3, & 4

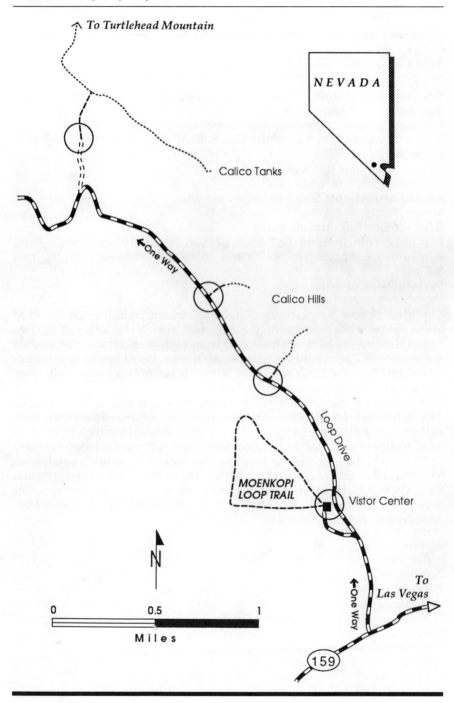

the new leaves. These leaves can lose well over half their water and still survive. In comparison, humans are seriously ill after a water loss of only a few percent.—*Bureau of Land Management and Bruce Grubbs*

HIKE 2 *CALICO HILLS*

General description: A short round-trip day hike in the Red Rock Canyon National Conservation Area.
General location: Approximately 15 miles west of Las Vegas.
Maps: La Madre Mtn 7.5-minute USGS, BLM brochure.
Difficulty: Easy.
Length: One mile one-way.
Elevation: 3,920 to 4,329 feet.
Special attractions: Slickrock sandstone hills.
Water: None.
Best season: Fall through spring.
For more information: Red Rock Canyon National Conservation Area, Bureau of Land Management, PO Box 26569, Las Vegas, NV 89126; (702) 363-1921.
Permit: None (day use only).

The hike: Follow the description under Moenkopi Trail to reach the BLM visitor center. Then continue on the loop road (one way) to either of the two Calico Hills overlooks. Short trails lead from each overlook into the wash at the base of the Calico Hills. From the wash it is easy to scramble up the sandstone hills. Seasonal pools are found in the rock. This very easy walk gives one a quick idea of the nature of slickrock.

The origin and exact meaning of the term slickrock is unclear. It is generally used in the American Southwest to describe areas of exposed sandstone such as this. From a distance the term is descriptive, because in arid climates sandstone erodes to form sleekly rounded domes and turrents. Up close, the hiker will discover that the rock is anything but slick. It is nature's sandpaper, composed of billions of grains of sand cemented together by heat and pressure. Contrary to popular opinion, slickrock country is primarily eroded by water during the rare desert storms. Wind plays a very minor role.—*Bureau of Land Management and Bruce Grubbs.*

Slickrock sandstone forms a complex topography more typical of Utah in the Calico Hills, part of the Red Rock Recreation Lands near Las Vegas.

HIKE 3 *CALICO TANKS*

General description: A round-trip day hike in the Red Rock Canyon National Conservation Area.
General location: Approximately fifteen miles west of Las Vegas.
Maps: La Madre Mtn 7.5-minute USGS, BLM brochure.
Difficulty: Moderate.
Length: 1.3 miles one-way.
Elevation: 4,280 to 4,700 feet.
Special attractions: Natural water tanks.
Water: Seasonal in tanks.
Best season: Fall through spring.
For more information: Red Rock Canyon National Conservation Area, Bureau of Land Management, PO Box 26569, Las Vegas, NV 89126; (702) 363-1921.
Permit: None (day use only).

The hike: Follow the description under Moenkopi Trail to reach the BLM visitor center. Then continue on the loop road (one way) to Sandstone Quarry and park. Follow the wash north 0.25 miles, then turn right (east) at the third canyon and continue up a side canyon to a large natural water tank (tinaja). When they have water, this and other tinajas in the Calico Hills are important sources of water for the area's wildlife.

Tinaja is Spanish for "tank". Most natural desert water tanks are smaller than this one, and tend to form where cascading flood waters have scoured out deep basins in the rock. They tend to occur in deep canyons where the additional shade helps keep the water from evaporating. In many desert ranges, tinajas are the only year round source of water for wildlife. Hikers can use the water as well, but should observe a few courtesies. Take only the water you need, and use it sparingly for all purposes except drinking. Never bath in a tinaja or pollute it with soap or food scraps. Others will need the water. Avoid camping nearby, as your presence will scare away the animals which normally come to drink during the night. Finally, water from a tinaja should always be purified before drinking or cooking with it.—*Bureau of Land Management and Bruce Grubbs*

HIKE 4 *TURTLEHEAD PEAK*

General description: A round-trip day hike in the Red Rock Canyon National Conservation Area.

General location: Approximately fifteen miles west of Las Vegas. Maps: La Madre Mtn 7.5-minute USGS, BLM brochure.

Difficulty: Difficult.

Length: 2.5 miles one-way.

Elevation: 4,280 to 6,324 feet.

Special attractions: Spectacular views.

Water: None.

Best season: Fall through spring.

For more information: Red Rock Canyon National Conservation Area, Bureau of Land Management, PO Box 26569, Las Vegas, NV 89126; (702) 363-1921.

Permit: None (day use only).

The hike: Follow the description under Moenkopi Trail to reach the BLM visitor center. Then continue on the loop road (one way) to Sandstone Quarry and park. This route follows a wash north through the Calico Hills, climbs a revine to the left of Turtlehead, and follows the ridge to the top. The spectacular views are well worth the long climb.

From the summit you can see a representative sample of the Mojave Desert, which encompasses the southern tip of Nevada, most of southeastern California, and a bit of western Arizona. The Mojave's symbol is the Joshua Tree, a large yucca. Joshua Trees tend to grow on the higher slopes of the valleys, with creosote bush dominating at lower elevations, a yucca belt at higher elevations, and above the yuccas, a pinyon life zone where the dominate plants are the pinyon pines and juniper trees.—*Bureau of Land Management and Bruce Grubbs*

HIKE 5 *KEYSTONE THRUST*

General description: A round-trip day hike in the Red Rock Canyon National Conservation Area.
General location: Approximately fifteen miles west of Las Vegas.
Maps: La Madre Mtn 7.5-minute USGS, BLM brochure.
Difficulty: Easy.
Length: Two miles one-way.
Elevation: 4,800 to 5,300 feet.
Special attractions: Keystone Thrust Fault contact zone.
Water: None.
Best season: Fall through spring.
For more information: Red Rock Canyon National Conservation Area, Bureau of Land Management, PO Box 26569, Las Vegas, NV 89126; (702) 363-1921.
Permit: None (day use only).

The hike: Follow the description under Moenkopi Trail to reach the BLM visitor center. Then continue on the loop road (one way) to the lower White Rock Springs parking area and park. Follow the the dirt road 0.8 mile to a closed dirt road on the right (east). Follow the trail approximately 0.75 mile to the fork, and follow the right fork down to the small canyon and the contact of the Keystone Thrust Fault.

A thrust fault is a fracture in the earth's crust where one rock plate is thrust horizontally over another. Normally younger rocks are found on top of older rocks, as they are deposited in layered succession. But here the older limestone has been pushed over the top of the younger sandstone. It is believed that this occurred about sixty-five million years ago when two continental plates collided to create the present North American continent. The thrust contact is clearly defined by the sharp contrast between the gray limestones and the red sandstones. The Keystone Thrust Fault extends from the Cottonwood Fault (along the Pahrump Highway) thirteen miles northward to the vicinity of La Madre Mountain where it is obscured by more complex faulting.—*Bureau of Land Management*

HIKES 5, 6, 7, 8, 9, & 13

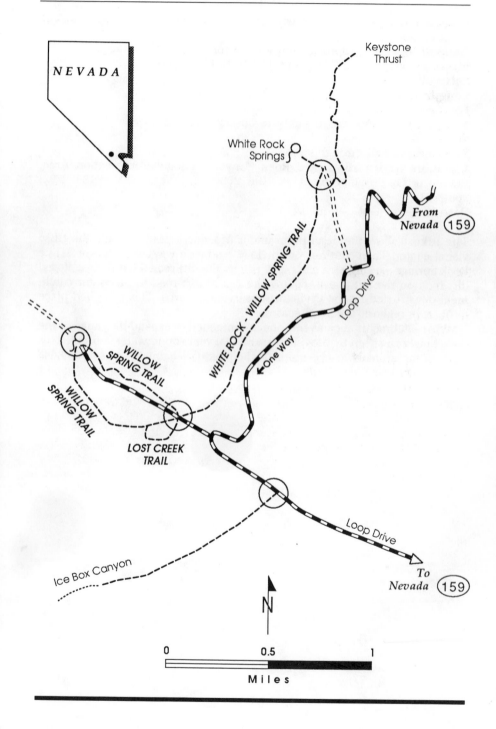

NEVADA

Keystone Thrust

White Rock Springs

From Nevada (159)

Loop Drive

WHITE ROCK - WILLOW SPRING TRAIL

One Way

WILLOW SPRING TRAIL

WILLOW SPRING TRAIL

LOST CREEK TRAIL

Ice Box Canyon

Loop Drive

To Nevada (159)

N

0   0.5   1

Miles

HIKE 6 *WHITE ROCK SPRING*

General description: A round-trip day hike in the Red Rock Canyon National Conservation Area.

General location: Approximately fifteen miles west of Las Vegas.

Maps: La Madre Mtn 7.5-minute USGS, BLM brochure.

Difficulty: Easy.

Length: One mile one-way.

Elevation: 4,800 feet.

Special attractions: Opportunity to observe bighorn sheep.

Water: None.

Best season: Fall through spring.

For more information: Red Rock Canyon National Conservation Area, Bureau of Land Management, PO Box 26569, Las Vegas, NV 89126; (702) 363-1921.

Permit: None (day use only).

The hike: Follow the description under Moenkopi Trail to reach the BLM visitor center. Then continue on the loop road (one way) to the lower White Rock Springs parking area and park. Follow the dirt road 0.9 mile to a closed dirt road on the left (west). Follow the closed dirt road to the water catchment constructed by the Civilian Conservation Corps. This is a good place to observe bighorn sheep, in season.

Water catchments such as this one are intended to expand the range of the desert bighorn sheep by providing additional year round water sources. This enables the animals to use more of their natural habitat.—*Bureau of Land Management and Bruce Grubbs*

HIKE 7 *WHITE ROCK SPRING TO WILLOW SPRING*

General description: A round-trip day hike in the Red Rock Canyon National Conservation Area.
General location: Approximately fifteen miles west of Las Vegas.
Maps: La Madre Mtn 7.5-minute USGS, BLM brochure.
Difficulty: Easy.
Length: 1.5 miles one-way.
Elevation: 4,800 to 4,400 feet.
Special attractions: Connection between White Spring & Willow Spring trails.
Water: None.
Best season: Fall through spring.
For more information: Red Rock Canyon National Conservation Area, Bureau of Land Management, PO Box 26569, Las Vegas, NV 89126; (702) 363-1921.
Permit: None (day use only).

The hike: Follow the description under Moenkopi Trail to reach the BLM visitor center. Then continue on the loop road (one way) to the lower White Rock Springs parking area and park. Follow the dirt road 0.9 mile to a closed dirt road on the left (west). Follow the closed dirt road to the water catchment. Just before reaching the catchment the trail to Willow Spring can be located on the left, heading in a southwesterly direction. The trail follows along the base of the White Rock Hills, and joins the Willow Spring Trail across from the Lost Creek parking area.

Along this trail or almost anywhere in the Nevada desert you are likely to see one of the American desert's most common mammals; the jackrabbit with its large, black tipped ears. It is commonly seen bounding across roads and in good years is extremely numerous. The large ears contain many blood vessels and serve to radiate heat to the environment.—*Bureau of Land Management and Bruce Grubbs*

HIKE 8 *LOST CREEK LOOP*

General description: A short loop day hike in the Red Rock Canyon National Conservation Area.

General location: Approximately fifteen miles west of Las Vegas.

Maps: La Madre Mtn 7.5-minute USGS, BLM brochure.

Difficulty: Easy.

Length: 0.7 miles round trip.

Elevation: 4,400 feet.

Special attractions: Box canyon with a seasonal waterfall.

Water: Lost Creek.

Best season: Fall through spring.

For more information: Red Rock Canyon National Conservation Area, Bureau of Land Management, PO Box 26569, Las Vegas, NV 89126; (702) 363-1921.

Permit: None (day use only).

The hike: Follow the description under Moenkopi Trail to reach the BLM visitor center. Then continue on the loop road (one way) to the Lost Creek parking area and park. Take either the right or left loop to the creek, with its permanent water. One can continue upstream to a box canyon with a seasonal waterfall.

A box canyon is a canyon with no outlet at its upper end. Usually the obstacle is a dry waterfall which runs only occasionally.—*Bureau of Land Management and Bruce Grubbs*

HIKE 9 *WILLOW SPRING LOOP*

General description: A loop day hike in the Red Rock Canyon National Conservation Area.
General location: Approximately fifteen miles west of Las Vegas.
Maps: La Madre Mtn 7.5-minute USGS, BLM brochure.
Difficulty: Easy.
Length: 1.5 miles round trip.
Elevation: 4,400 feet.
Special attractions: Variety of plant communities-riparian, pines, oaks and desert.
Water: Willow Spring.
Best season: Fall through spring.
For more information: Red Rock Canyon National Conservation Area, Bureau of Land Management, PO Box 26569, Las Vegas, NV 89126; (702) 363-1921.
Permit: None (day use only).

The hike: Follow the description under Moenkopi Trail to reach the BLM visitor center. Then continue on the loop road (one way) to the Willow Spring Picnic Area and park. The trail follows the left (northeast) side of the canyon past Native American roasting pits to the Lost Creek parking area. The right hand trail then crosses Red Rock Wash, branches to the right, and parallels the Red Rock Escarpment and returns to Willow Spring.

Roasting pits were used by the ancient inhabitants for slow-cooking. Agave plants, other vegetables, and meats were placed in a bed of hot coals mixed with cobbles and covered with plant materials and earth. After enough time had passed, the cooked food, ash, and fire cracked rock were dug out. The discarded rock and ash forms a doughnut shaped ring often several feet high. Also known as mescal pits, these cooking sites are common in the Southwest.— *Bureau of Land Management and Bruce Grubbs*

HIKE 10 *LA MADRE SPRING*

General description: A round-trip day hike in the Red Rock Canyon National Conservation Area.
General location: Approximately fifteen miles west of Las Vegas.
Maps: La Madre Mtn 7.5-minute, La Madre Spring 7.5-minute, Mountain Springs 15-minute USGS, BLM brochure.
Difficulty: Moderate.
Length: Two miles one-way trip.
Elevation: 4,400 to 5,360 feet.
Special attractions: Opportunity to view bighorn sheep and other wildlife.
Water: Le Madre Spring.
Best season: Fall through spring.
For more information: Red Rock Canyon National Conservation Area, Bureau of Land Management, PO Box 26569, Las Vegas, NV 89126; (702) 363-1921.
Permit: None (day use only).

The hike: Follow the description under Moenkopi Trail to reach the BLM visitor center. Then continue on the loop road (one way) to the Willow Spring Picnic Area and park. Hike up the Rocky Gap road, a jeep road which begins at the end of the pavement. Watch for the right fork in the road past the wash and follow it to the dam. A foot path leads up the creek to the spring. Bighorn sheep and other wildlife rely on the water from this spring.

The Red Rock country is home to a number of snakes, including rattlesnakes. Since they can cause serious injury, these poisonous snakes should be treated with great respect, but as mentioned under *Making it a Safe Trip,* a few simple precautions will reduce the chance of being bitten to almost zero. Once fear of the unknown is dispelled, rattlesnakes become fascinating animals.

Although many people think of rattlesnakes as denizens of scorching hot and totally barren deserts, they actually prefer areas where their principal food is found, which is small mammals and birds. Since springs attract their prey, rattlesnakes become more abundant as well. As with all reptiles, their body takes on the temperature of their environment. Since they are most active and comfortable when their body temperature is in the eighties, rattlesnakes tend to prefer shady areas in hot weather, and sunny areas in cool wheather.

Several species are found in southern Nevada. The most widespread is the Great Basin rattlesnake, a subspecies of the Western rattlesnake. This is the northern limits of the Mojave rattlesnake, which has the most potent venom of all rattlesnakes. And finally, early on summer mornings in sandy areas, you may encounter the peculiar S-shaped tracks of the sidewinder. This small rattlesnake has developed a unique sideways method of motion to make movement possible in the sandy environment it prefers.—*Bureau of Land Management and Bruce Grubbs*

HIKE 11 *TOP OF THE ESCARPMENT*

General description: A round-trip day hike in the Red Rock Canyon National Conservation Area.
General location: Approximately fifteen miles west of Las Vegas.
Maps: La Madre Mtn 7.5-minute, La Madre Spring 7.5- minute, Mountain Springs 15-minute USGS, BLM brochure.
Difficulty: Difficult.
Length: Five miles one-way.
Elevation: 4,400 to 7,500 feet.
Special attractions: Excellent views of the Red Rock Escarpment.
Water: None.
Best season: Fall thru Spring.
For more informations: Red Rock Canyon National Conservation Area, Bureau of Land Management, PO Box 26569, Las Vegas, NV 89126; (702) 363-1921.
Permit: Registration required for overnight use.
Finding the trailhead: Follow the description under Moenkopi Trail to reach the BLM visitor center. Then continue on the loop road (one way) to the Willow Spring Picnic Area and park. Hike up the Rocky Gap road, a jeep trail which begins at the end of the pavement. Watch for the left (southwest) fork. This four-wheel drive road passes Lone Pine and Switchback Springs as it climbs to Red Rock Summit.

If the road is impassable From Red Rock Summit then about five miles and 3000 feet elevation gain will be added to the hike to reach Red Rock Summit. Alternately, Red Rock Summit may be approached from the west. From Las Vegas, drive twenty-seven miles west on NV 160 to Mountain Springs. Continue about three miles, then turn right (north) on the Lovell Canyon road. In approximately eight miles, the road to Red Rock Summit turns right (east). It is about three miles and 1200 feet elevation gain to the summit.

The hike: The trail begins at Red Rock Summit and leaves the road to the east. It winds up around the head of a basin that drains to the west, and eventually reaches the summit of the escarpment after a mile walk with approximately 700 feet of elevation gain. From the summit the view encompasses the Spring Mountains to the north, the entire Red Rocks, Blue Diamond Mountain, the Las Vegas Valley, Lake Mead and the Mormon Mountains and Mount Potosi. Now follow the ridge east-northeast to a spectacular viewpoint overlooking the Red Rocks.—*Bureau of Land Management*

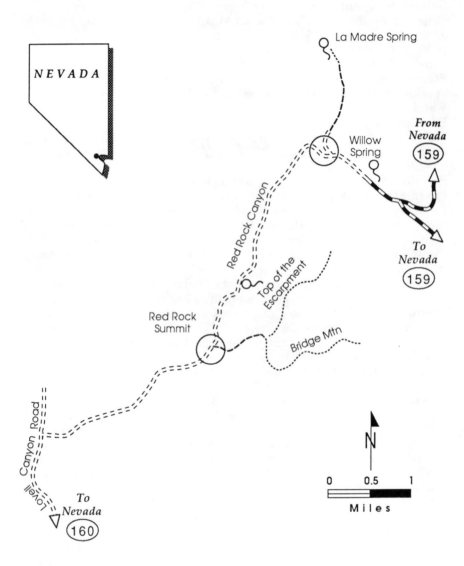

NEVADA

La Madre Spring

Willow Spring

From Nevada
(159)

To Nevada
(159)

Red Rock Canyon

Top of the Escarpment

Red Rock Summit

Bridge Mtn

Lovell Canyon Road

To Nevada
(160)

N

0   0.5   1

Miles

HIKE 12 *BRIDGE MOUNTAIN*

General description: A round-trip day hike in the Red Rock Canyon National Conservation Area.

General location: Approximately fifteen miles west of Las Vegas.

Maps: Mountain Springs 15-minute, La Madre Mtn 7.5- minute, La Madre Spring 7.5-minute USGS, BLM brochure.

Difficulty: Difficult.

Length: Seven miles one way.

Elevation: 4,400 to 7,500 feet (3,800 foot elevation change).

Special attractions: Natural bridge, views of Red Rock Canyon area.

Water: Seasonal in potholes.

Best season: Spring through fall.

For more information: Red Rock Canyon National Conservation Area, Bureau of Land Management, PO Box 26569, Las Vegas, NV 89126; (702) 363-1921.

Permit: Registration required for overnight use.

Special Instructions: Although this is a day hike of moderate length, the trail is minimal, and the last 400 foot climb to the natural bridge on Bridge Mountain is along a steep exposed system of joints and ledges. This section does not require technical climbing equipment or skills, but does require extreme care. Only hikers experienced in cross-country travel should attempt this hike.

Finding the trailhead: For access to the trail head see the Top of the Escarpment description.

The hike: The trail begins at Red Rock Summit and leaves the road to the east. It winds up around the head of a basin that drains to the west, and eventually reaches the summit of the escarpment after a mile walk with approximately 700 feet of elevation gain.

Now the trail turns south along the ridge line for approximately 0.25 mile. It descends around the heads of two small drainages to the east then climbs a steep side hill to the top of a long narrow ridge that runs off to the east into Pine Creek. No trail exists in the resistant sandstone, but the route is intermittently marked by two black parallel lines of paint.

This ridge offers an excellent view of the famous Keystone Thrust Fault Zone. Tremendous forces associated with the movement of the Earth's crustal plates have forced the dark gray limestones to ride up over the red and white sandstones that were formed later, and were originally positioned above the limestone. The limestone weathers into fairly large blocks that remain in place, trapping sand, silt and plant debris which develops into soil that supports a heavy cover of shrubs and small trees. The sandstone weathers differently, breaking down into sand grains that are easily washed and blown away, constantly exposing a new surface of solid rock that is bare of all plants except lichens and a few shrubs growing in cracks. The contrast between the brush covered limestone and the bare sandstone beneath it clearly delineates the Keystone Thrust Fault Zone.

The trail becomes poorly defined as it snakes down the crest of the ridge to the east. Hikers should stay on the crest as much as possible as the going is easier there than it is on the side hill. Soon after the limestone rock disappears and exposes the sandstone, the route drops off the ridge to the north into a small basin that empties into Pine Creek. At the lower edge of the basin a sheer cliff descends into the depths of Pine Creek 1,500 feet below. Rising air currents are attractive to soaring birds which ride along the cliffs, and the rising air also carries flying insects to the higher elevations. Small insect-eating birds such as the White-Throated Swift and Violet Green Swallow swoop along the edge, buzzing hikers and snapping up bugs on the wing.

From the head of Pine Creek the route winds off through a slickrock bench studded with numerous small catch basins that hold water after a rain. Some of these basins are quite large; the largest is located in the extreme southeast corner of section 8, near the edge of the Mountain Springs quad. Water trapped in these tanks, or tinajas as the Spanish termed them, supports a diverse and fragile community of plants and animals. Ponderosa pines, junipers, pinyon pines and smaller bushes provide shelter for bird life. Amphibians such as frogs and toads breed in the ponds, and ravens, hawks, deer, bighorn sheep and hundreds of other animals rely on the tinajas for water. People should never camp within 0.25 mile of such water sources as the presence of humans will scare the wildlife away. Since there is no outlet from the tanks, pollutants from soap, human wastes, or litter will remain in the basins indefinitely, poisoning the creatures that depend on these natural reservoirs.

From the large tank mentioned above, the trail becomes a mere route across the slickrock bench. The correct route is marked intermittently with small patches of orange paint in the shape of bighorn sheep tracks. If the correct route is not followed carefully, hikers will find themselves perched on the edge of a sheer drop with no way down. In many areas the route is broken by short vertical pitches that must be carefully negotiated. It is approximately 0.5 mile from the big tank to the bottom of the saddle that leads up to Bridge Mountain, with a drop of 350 feet.

To reach the bridge near the summit of Bridge Mountain the route leads straight up a system of joints and ledges for a distance of 400 feet. The path is not as sheer as it appears during the approach, and there are plenty of holds for hands and feet. However, the climb is relatively exposed, and extreme care should be exercised during the climb. A misstep could plunge a hiker hundreds of feet into Pine Creek. Climbing within the joints offers more security, but climbing the faces alongside is slightly easier.

Once the bridge has been reached and explored, a further route leads up onto the bench above, from inside the alcove near the pine tree. Just one hundred yards north of the bridge is a large, deep, nearly circular tinaja nearly eighty feet across and sixty feet deep. Over the bench to the east is a large alcove that shelters a hidden forest of ponderosa pines. Trees grow very slowly in this area because of the dry conditions. Wood is relatively scarce, slowly replaced and absolutely should not be used to build fires. A fire in the hidden forest could cause damage that would not heal in a thousand years. Note that all wood gathering and ground fires are prohibited in the Red Rock backcountry.

Return to Red Rock Summit by retracing your route. Do not attempt to take short cuts or alternate routes.—*Bureau of Land Management*

HIKE 13 ICE BOX CANYON

General description: A round-trip day hike in the Red Rock Canyon National Conservation Area.

General location: Approximately twenty miles west of Las Vegas.

Maps: La Madre Mtn 7.5-minute, Mountain Springs 15- minute USGS, BLM brochure.

Difficulty: Easy.

Length: 1.3 miles one-way.

Elevation: 4,300 to 4,600 feet.

Special attractions: Seasonal waterfall and box canyon.

Water: None.

Best season: Spring through fall.

For more information: Red Rock Canyon National Conservation Area, Bureau of Land Management, PO Box 26569, Las Vegas, NV 89126; (702) 363-1921.

Permit: None (day use only)

The hike: Follow the description under Moenkopi Trail to reach the BLM visitor center. Then continue on the loop road (one way) to the Ice Box Canyon Overlook and park. Follow the trail across the wash. The trail stays on the the bench on the right (north) side of the canyon until the canyon narrows, and then ends as it drops into the wash. Follow the wash (boulder hopping is required) to a seasonal waterfall and box canyon. Ice Box Canyon derives its name from the cooler temperatures in this narrow canyon.

These cooler temperatures create what are called micro climates, small areas where the year round climate is different enough from the surrounding area to support a plant and animal community normally found at higher elevations.—*Bureau of Land Management and Bruce Grubbs*

An excellent trail leads into Pine Creek Canyon in the Red Rock Recreation Lands.

HIKE 14 *PINE CREEK CANYON*

General description: A round-trip day hike in the Red Rock Canyon National Conservation Area.
General location: Approximately 20 miles west of Las Vegas.
Maps: Blue Diamond 7.5-minute, La Madre Mtn 7.5- minute, Mountain Springs 15-minute USGS, BLM brochure.
Difficulty: Moderate.
Length: 2.5 miles one-way.
Elevation: 4,000 to 5,000 feet.
Special attractions: Unusual low-elevation pine forest.
Water: None.
Best season: Spring through fall.
For more information: Red Rock Canyon National Conservation Area, Bureau of Land Management, PO Box 26569, Las Vegas, NV 89126; (702) 363-1921.
Permit: None (day use only).

The hike: Follow the description under Moenkopi Trail to reach the BLM visitor center. Then continue on the loop road (one way) to the Pine Creek Canyon Overlook and park. Follow the trail downhill to the closed dirt road which leads to the old Horace Wilson homestead site; nothing remains except the foundation. The canyon divides above the homestead site; either fork can be followed but the left is preferable. Pine Creek was named for the unusual occurrence of ponderosa pines at this elevation in the desert the trees thrive here because of the moisture and cooler temperatures.

Here the micro climate supporting the tall pines is caused by the high canyon walls which increase the amount of shade, the moisture from the Pine Creek drainage, and the cool air flowing down the canyon at night. After sunset on calm clear nights, the ground in the high mountains rapidly cools by radiating its heat to the open sky. This in turn cools the air in contact with the earth. The cool air is heavier than warmer air and starts to flow downward, collecting in the drainages and moving toward the valleys via the canyons. This is why there is often a down canyon breeze or even a wind in desert canyons and mountain valleys after sunset.—*Bureau of Land Management and Burce Grubbs*

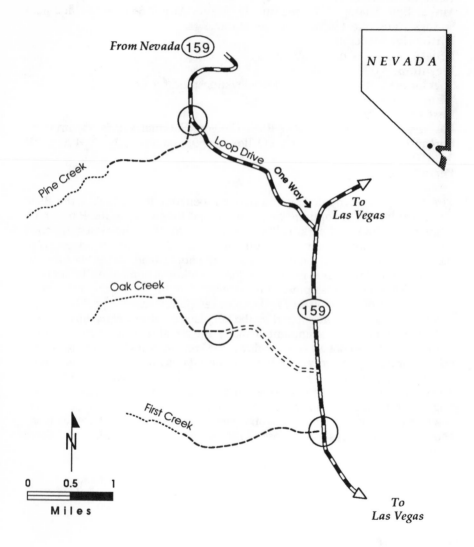

HIKE 15 *OAK CREEK CANYON*

General description: A round-trip day hike in the Red Rock Canyon National Conservation Area.

General location: Approximately twenty miles west of Las Vegas.

Maps: Blue Diamond 7.5-minute USGS, BLM brochure.

Difficulty: Moderate.

Length: Three miles one-way.

Elevation: 3,760 to 4,800 feet.

Special attractions: Stands of Live Shrub Oak, sandy "beaches" along the wash.

Water: None.

Best season: Spring through fall.

For more information: Red Rock Canyon National Conservation Area, Bureau of Land Management, PO Box 26569, Las Vegas, NV 89126; (702) 363-1921.

Permit: None (day use only).

The hike: Follow the description under Moenkopi Trail to reach the scenic loop entry, but stay on NV 159 south 1.6 miles past the scenic loop exit, and turn right (west) onto the dirt road and park. Follow the road (very rough four-wheel drive) to the road closure at its end. Now follow the trail around "Potato Knoll" to the left. Oak Creek Canyon is known for its nice stands of Live Shrub Oak and the sandy "beaches" along the wash. Seasonal waterfalls can be found in the canyon.

The term "live oak" means that the plant is evergreen and keeps its leaves all year. Shrub oaks often grow in thick stands with mountain mahogany and manzanita, creating formidable obstacles to cross country hikers. However, the dense brush provides important cover for wildlife.—*Bureau of Land Management and Bruce Grubbs*

HIKE 16 *FIRST CREEK CANYON*

General description: A round-trip day hike in the Red Rock Canyon National Conservation Area.

General location: Approximately twenty miles west of Las Vegas.

Maps: Blue Diamond 7.5-minute, Mountain Springs 15- minute USGS, BLM brochure.

Difficulty: Moderate.

Length: 2.5 miles one-way.

Elevation: 3,650 to 4,800 feet.

Special attractions: Scenic canyon with seasonal waterfalls.

Water: None.

Best season: Spring through fall.

For more information: Red Rock Canyon National Conservation Area, Bureau of Land Management, PO Box 26569, Las Vegas, NV 89126; (702) 363-1921.

Permit: None (day use only).

The hike: Follow the description under Moenkopi Trail to reach the scenic loop entry, but stay on NV 159 south 2.6 miles past the scenic loop exit and park in the large dirt parking area. Follow the closed dirt road to the mouth of the canyon. A trail follows the left side of the canyon for a distance; some rock scrambling is required thereafter.

Seasonal waterfalls are found all over Nevada in the numberless canyons that cut into the flanks of the mountains. At higher elevations the falls run during the snowmelt during late spring and early summer, and sometimes briefly after heavy thunderstorms. At lower elevations such as these runoff tends to occur during wet storms, which primarily occur in winter. The best chance to see the falls running is in late winter or early spring.—*Bureau of Land Management and Bruce Grubbs*

HIKE 17 *CHARLESTON PEAK LOOP TRAIL*

General description: A long loop day hike in the Spring Mountains.
General location: Approximately forty-one miles northwest of Las Vegas.
Maps: Charleston Peak 15-minute USGS quad; Toiyabe National Forest USFS.
Difficulty: Difficult.
Length: 13 miles.
Elevation: 7,700 to 11,918 feet.
Special attractions: Alpine ridge hike with spectacular alpine views.
Water: Spring on Mummy Mountain.
Best season: Summer through fall.
For more information: Toiyabe National Forest, 550 E. Las Vegas Blvd., Las Vegas, NV 89104; (702) 388-6255.
Permit: None.
Special instructions: Caution should be used if attempting this hike in late spring or early summer as the higher sections of the trail may be covered with snow, especially the North Loop near Charleston Peak. It may not be possible to traverse the steep slopes safely without climbing equipment.
Finding the trailhead: From Las Vegas, drive northwest on US 95 approximately thirteen miles and turn left (west) on the signed and paved Kyle Canyon Road, NV 157. Continue nineteen miles to the summer home area, then continue straight on Echo Road (NV 157 turns sharply left and crosses the creek). After 0.5 mile, turn right (staying on Echo Road) and go 0.1 mile to the North Loop trail head.

The hike: The loop hike ends at the South Loop trail head, 1.5 miles away. To drive to the South Loop Trailhead, stay on NV 157 to its end at the Cathedral Rock Picnic Area; the trailhead is within the picnic area and is signed.

The North Loop trail climbs steeply up a drainage as it heads toward the crest of the range. A beautiful forest of ponderosa pine and quaking aspen gives way to a more open view in an old burn on the southwest slopes of Mummy Mountain. A series of switchbacks lead to the unsigned junction with the Deer Creek Trail in a saddle. Swinging northwest, the trail climbs across Mummy Mountain past the spring shown on the topographic map. After the spring the trail swings southwest and west and gradually climbs to the crest, where there are views of the Lee Canyonarea to the north.

Staying near the crest but skirting peaks to the left, the trail traverses limestone slopes forested with bristlecone pine and finally reaches the slopes of Sharleston Peak, where it switchbacks up the east slopes to the summit.

The South Loop trail descends the treeless west slopes of the peak from just north of the summit, then follows the long, nearly level crest through a fine bristlecone forest. About 0.5 mile before reaching peak 11,072, the trail turns left (north) at the signed junction with the Lovell Canyon trail, and descends via many switchbacks toward the floor of Kyle Canyon. Near the bottom, the trail drops inbto a drainage to avoid high limestone cliffs; this spectacular area is a major snow avalanche path in winter. Notice that there are few trees in the drainage, and the trees near the sides are all of the same size and age. This is due to the regular occurrence of snow slides which destroy the trees.

The South Mount Charleston Loop Trail in the Spring Mountains provides excellent views, staying at 11,000 feet for more than six miles.

HIKE 17 *CHARLESTON PEAK LOOP TRAIL*

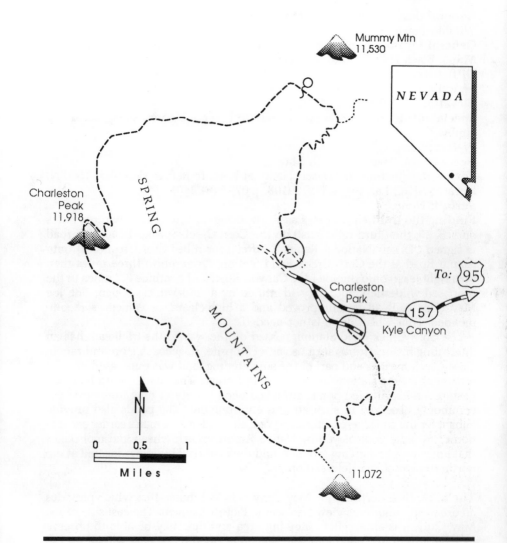

At the bottom of the drainage there is a choice of a left and right fork; stay right on the newer trail. At the picnic area it is easy to walk up the road to the North Loop trail head.—*Bruce Grubbs*

HIKE 18 *JOE MAY CANYON*

General description: A remote round-trip day hike in the Desert National Wildlife Range.

General location: Approximately thirty-five miles north of Las Vegas.

Maps: Black Hills 7.5-minute, Corn Creek Springs 7.5- minute USGS quads.

Difficulty: Moderate.

Length: 3.4 miles one way.

Elevation: 4,800 to 6,861 feet.

Special attractions: Good opportunity to observe bighorn sheep, including lambs.

Water: None.

Best season: March through May.

For more information: Desert National Wildlife Refuge Complex, 1500 N. Decatur Blvd., Las Vegas, NV 89108; (702) 646- 3401.

Permit: None.

Finding the trailhead: From Las Vegas, drive northwest twenty-three miles on U.S. 95, then turn right (east) on the Corn Creek Springs Road (this road is signed "Desert National Range"). After four miles turn left (north) onto Alamo Road at the Corn Creek Field Station. Drive north three miles then turn right (east) onto the Joe May Canyon Road and continue 3.7 miles to the proposed wilderness boundary, identified by a "No Vehicles" sign. The Joe May Canyon Road is unimproved and a high-clearance vehicle is recommended. Four-wheel drive is not needed.

The Corn Creek Field Station, passed on the way to the trailhead, has an interesting history. It has seen use as a campsite, stagecoach stop, and ranch. Corn Creek Springs and part of the surrounding land was purchased in 1939 for use as a field station for the Wildlife Refuge. The station, with its trees, pasture, and spring fed ponds attracts a wide variety of migrating birds not commonly observed in such an arid environment. The ponds also provide habitat for the endangered Pahrump poolfish. Evidence of man's earier occupation of this site is displayed by Native American arrowhead and tool flakes that litter the surrounding grounds, and the historical buildings located at the northern side of the field station.

The hike: Hike north up Joe May Canyon to Wildhorse Pass which provides an excellent panoramic view into scenic Picture Canyon. The east side of Joe May Canyon is an excellent lambing area and one may be able to observe large groups of ewes and lambs in this area. Good binoculars will be useful. About 1.5 miles from the "No Vehicles" sign is the Joe May Guzzler in a small side canyon. This is an example of one method used to develop water for bighorn sheep and other wildlife.

Desert bighorn sheep prefer rugged mountains and negotiate steep terrain with impressive agility for their somewhat bulky appearance. The size of a small deer, their gray brown color blends nicely with the desert tones, making them difficult to spot. Males are distinguished by their massive curling horns, while the females have much smaller horns. It is thought that the bighorns once ranged much more widely, but pressure from man has limited them to more rugged terrain. Although they cannot survive without liquid water, the

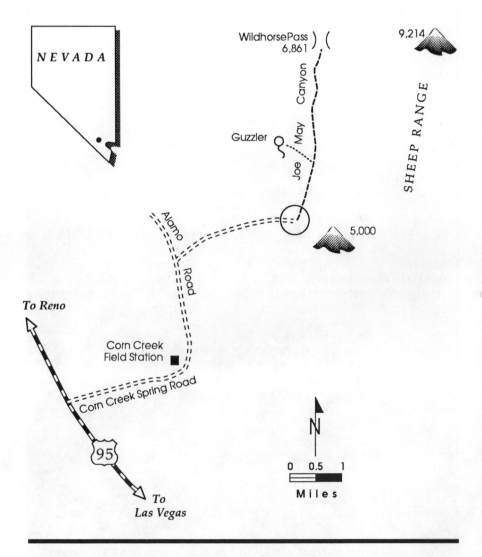

sheep do obtain enough moisture from green vegetation to enable them to go without water three to five days in hot weather, and ten to fourteen days in cold weather.—*US Fish and Wildlife Service and Bruce Grubbs*

The long Toiyabe Summit Trail traverses the spectacular south half of the Toiyabe Range, making it one of the longest trails in Nevada.

HIKE 19 *TOIYABE SUMMIT TRAIL*

General description: A five-day one-way backpack in the Toiyabe Range.
General location: Thirty-five miles south of Austin.
Maps: Millett Ranch 15-minute, North Shoshone Peak 15-minute, South Toiyabe Peak 7.5-minute, Carvers NW 7.5-minute USGS quads.
Difficulty: Difficult.
Length: Approximately thirty miles one way.
Elevation: 6,345 to 10,400 feet.
Special attractions: A unique crest trail featuring 100 mile alpine and desert views, aspens and alpine streams.
Water: Numerous creeks and springs.
Best season: Summer through fall.
For more information: Toiyabe National Forest, Main and 5th, Austin, NV 89310; (702) 964-2671.
Permit: None
Finding the trailhead: From Austin, drive east on US 50, then south on NV 376. Approximately twenty-seven miles from Austin, turn west on the dirt Kingston Creek road. Park eight miles from the highway at the head of a reservoir not shown on the topo, opposite an abandoned ranch. There is no trailhead sign, but the Summit Trail is obvious switchbacking up the slope to the south. The trip will require a car left at the southern trailhead, which is reached by continuing south on NV 376 to the dirt Summit Canyon Road, approximately forth-five miles from Austin. Drive west 2.2 miles to the mouth of the canyon.

The hike: Although depicted fairly accurately on the topo maps, the trail is old and receives little maintenance. Sections of old trail confuse the route, and some new roads not shown on the topographic maps have been built up some of the side canyons. The hiker should have the topo maps and some experience in off trail route finding.

During early summer, water is plentiful as most drainages and springs will be flowing, and there will be snow to melt along the higher sections. Late in the summer and into fall, it may be necessary to carry more water along the dryer sections, especially at the north end of the trip.

From 7,500 feet at the trailhead, the trail climbs steeply to the crest over several miles, and reaches the high point of the trip at a flat-topped section of ridge (10,400 feet). The trail stays along the crest until it descends into an aspen grove at the head of Washington Creek, where there is good camping.

South of Washington Creek, the trail traverses the northwest slopes of Toiyabe Range Peak. The 10,960 foot peak is an easy climb, and the views of the desert 6,000 feet below and the adjoining ranges are well worth the effort. Boundary Peak in the White Mountains, the highest point in Nevada, is visible far to the southwest.

Continuing on the trail, there is good camping in an aspen grove on the west ridge of Toiyabe Range Peak. To the south, the trail stays on the west side of the crest as it heads the numerous forks of San Juan and Tierney Creeks.

Lack of summer rain and a long cold winter make life difficult for trees in the Toiyabe Range.

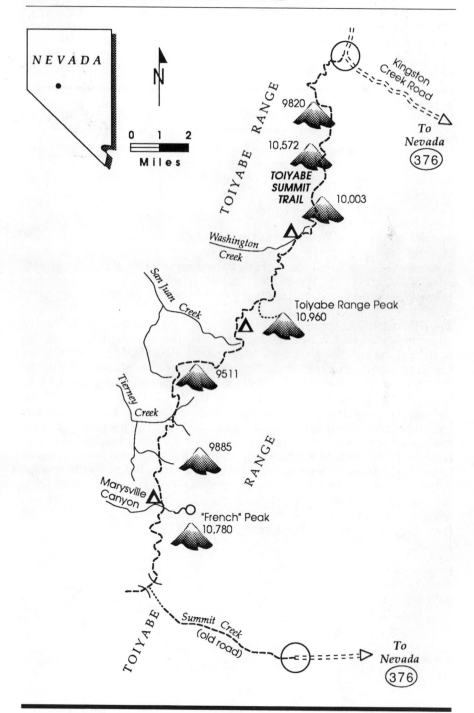

This is the faintest section of the trail and it may be lost occasionally. The spring at the head of Marysville Canyon provides good camping.

The trail south of "French" Peak (10,780 feet) is clearer. At the saddle at the head of Summit Canyon, descend cross-country through the the sage about 0.7 mile to the road in Summit Canyon, then follow the road down the spectacular canyon to its mouth.—*Bruce Grubbs*

HIKE 20 *COLD SPRINGS PONY EXPRESS STATION*

General description: A round-trip day hike trail to a Pony Express station.
General location: Fifty-one miles west of Austin.
Maps: Cold Springs 7.5-minute USGS quad.
Difficulty: Easy.
Length: 1.5 miles one-way.
Elevation: 5,480 to 5,800 feet.
Special attractions: Scenic views of Desatoya Mountains, Pony Express Historic Site.
For more information: Bureau of Land Management, 1535 Hot Springs Road, Suite 300, Carson City, NV 89706; (702) 885-6100.
Permit: None.

The hike: The Cold Springs Trail begins near U.S. 50 at an interpretive display which describes the Pony Express. The Pony Express delivered mail by horseback during 1860-1861 from Missouri to California. This trail provides access to a well- preserved Pony Express station. Other historic sites in the vicinity include an Overland Stage and a Transcontinental Telegraph station.

The Pony Express only operated for a year and a half but became famous for the speed and dangers of its service. Mail, at the rate of five dollars per half ounce, was carried nearly two thousand miles from St. Joseph to San Francisco in ten days by riders covering sixty to one-hundred miles at a full gallop. Stations were twenty-five miles apart, and the riders stopped only to change horses. Several station men and at least one rider were lost to hostile attacks. Advertisements for riders looked for young men without family ties, preferably orphans, who were willing to risk death daily. Late in 1861, the first successful telegraph message was sent between the same cities, ending the need for the Pony Express.—*Bureau of Land Management and Bruce Grubbs*

The southern Toiyabe Range stretches for miles in the crystal clear view from Toiyabe Range Peak. Visibilities of 150 miles are common.

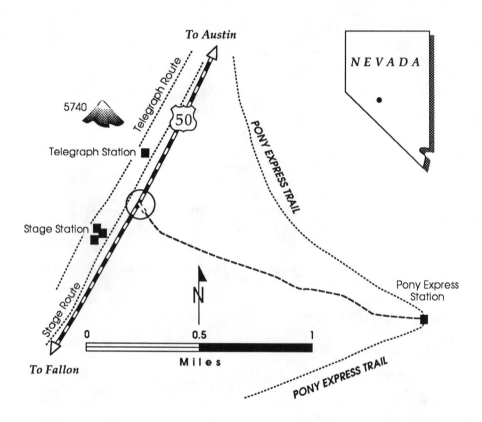

HIKE 21 SAND SPRINGS DESERT STUDY AREA

General description: Interpretive loop day hike through sand dune area.
General location: Twenty-three miles southeast of Fallon.
Map: Fourmile Flat 7.5-minute USGS quad.
Difficulty: Easy.
Length: One-half mile.
Elevation: 4,000 feet.
Special attractions: Pony Express station, sand dunes.
Water: None.
Best Season: September through May.
For more information: Bureau of Land Management, 1535 hot Springs Road, Suite 300, Carson City, NV 89706; (702) 885-6100.
Permit: None.

The hike: The Sand Springs Desert Study Area is located in a fifty acre area closed to off-road vehicles just south of Sand Mountain. Sand Mountain is approximately 3.5 miles long, one mile wide, and rises about 600 feet above the valley floor making it the largest single dune in the Great Basin. The interpretive trail is accessible by dirt road approximately 1.5 miles north of U.S. 50. The hiker can learn about the unique sand dune environment and view a Pony Express station along with other historic features.

Although many people unfamiliar with it think of the American desert as a vast area of sand dunes, the Sand Springs area is typical of sand dune areas in the Southwest. A particular combination of circumstances must combine before dunes are formed. There must be a supply of sand, prevailing winds tending to push the sand in the same direction, and a topographic feature acting as a trap to contain the sand. Here the surrounding mountains capture the wind blown grains.

It can be especially rewarding to explore the dunes at sunrise. The slanting sunlight emphasizes the texture of the surface and clearly shows the tracks and activities of animals active on the sand during the cool night hours.—
Bureau of Land Management and Bruce Grubbs

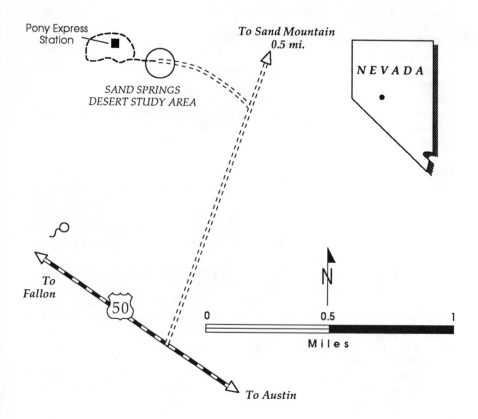

HIKE 22 GRIMES POINT ARCHAEOLOGICAL AREA

General description: A round-trip day hike on an interpretive trail.
General location: Ten miles east of Fallon.
Maps: Grimes Point 7.5-minute USGS quad.
Difficulty: Easy.
Length: About 1 mile.
Elevation: 4,000 to 4,200 feet.
Special Attractions: Petroglyphs, pictographs, rock shelters and caves.
Water: None.
Best Season: September through May.
For more information: Bureau of Land Management, 1535 hot Springs Road, Suite 300, Carson City, NV 89706; (702) 885-6100.
Permit: None.

The hike: The Grimes Point Archaeological Area contains two interpretive trails. The easy Petroglyph Trail is a short trail through a petroglyph boulder field. The longer Hidden Cave Trail provides access to petroglyphs, rock shelters and geological features. Hidden Cave is a major archaeological site used prehistorically by hunter-gatherers as a cache or storage site. The cave was occupied between 3,400 to 4,000 years ago.

Free public tours of the cave begin in Fallon at 10:00 a.m. on the second Saturday and fourth Saturday of each month. The trails are open to the public all year.

The Grimes Point Archaeological Site is located on U.S. 50 approximately ten miles east of Fallon. The Petroglyph Trail is located near the highway. The Hidden Cave Trail begins 1.5 miles north of the Grimes Point turnoff from U.S. 50, and access is via a well-maintained gravel road.

From the Grimes Point area, it is possible to see a series of horizontal lines on the distant mountains. These are wave terraces cut into the slopes by the waters of ancient Lake Lahontan, which reached depths of 700 feet. Although Grimes Point is a dry desolate area at present, 10,000 years ago it was a rich lakeshore, teeming with life. Given those conditions, it is not surprising that the ancient people spent a lot of time here.—*Bureau of Land Management and Bruce Grubbs*

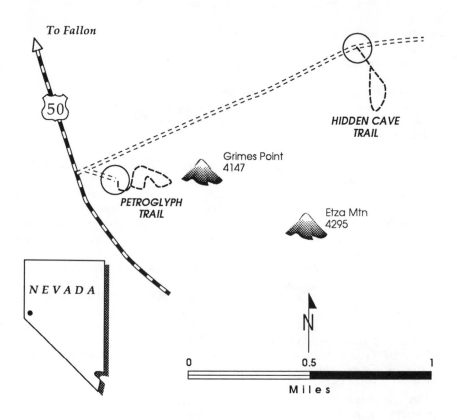

HIKE 23 *OPHIR CREEK TRAIL*

General description: A round-trip day hike in the Carson Range near Lake Tahoe.

General location: Two miles southwest of Washoe City.

Maps: Washoe City 7.5-minute, Mt. Rose 7.5-minute USGS quads.

Difficulty: Difficult.

Length: Six miles one-way.

Elevation: 5,300 to 8,600 feet.

Special attractions: Opportunity to view the results of a massive land slide.

Water: Water in Ophir Creek year round.

Best season: Spring through fall.

For more information: Toiyabe National Forest, 1536 S. Carson St., Carson City, NV 89701; (702) 882-2766.

Permit: None.

Finding the trailhead: To reach the lower (eastern) trailhead from Reno, drive south on US 395 and turn right one mile south of Washoe City. After 0.5 mile turn right to Davis Creek Park.

The hike: This hike is a difficult and strenuous climb up the Ophir Creek drainage to the remains of Upper and Lower Price Lakes which were destroyed when part of Slide Mountain fell into them in 1983. The resulting mud and water accumulation rushed down the Ophir Creek drainage and created a massive movement of earth that was deposited at Washoe Lake. It also removed part of the trail. Three miles from the western end, the trail turns into a jeep road which is open to hiking only. The last three miles parallel scenic Tahoe Meadows. The trail ends on Nevada Highway 431.

The tall pines with three long needles per bundle commonly found in the Carson Range and the Sierra Nevada are Jeffrey pine found in eastern and southern Nevada ranges, but are distinguished by the lighter color of their needles and by the unique strong smell of vanilla or lemon given off by crushed needles or twigs.—*US Forest Service and Bruce Grubbs*

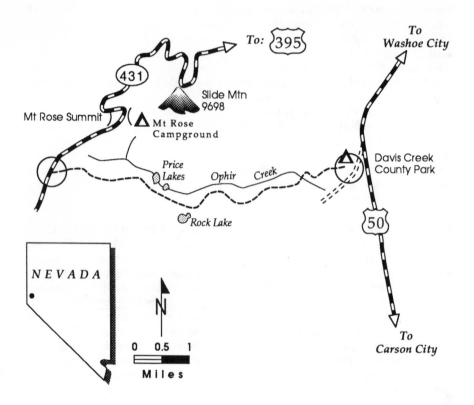

HIKE 24 *JONES CREEK-WHITES CREEK TRAIL*

General description: A loop day hike in the Carson Range.
General location: Approximately ten miles southwest of Reno.
Maps: Mt. Rose 7.5-minute, Mt. Rose NW 7.5-minute, Mt. Rose NE 7.5-minute, Washoe City 7.5-minute USGS quads.
Difficulty: Moderate to difficult.
Length: Eight miles one-way.
Elevation: 6,200 to 8,300 feet.
Special attractions: Outstanding views.
Water: Water in both Jones and Whites creek year-round.
Best season: Summer through fall.
For more information: Toiyabe National Forest, 1536 S. Carson St., Carson City, NV 89701; (702) 882-2766.
Permit: None.
Finding the trailhead: From Reno, drive eight miles south on US 395, then turn right (west) on NV 431. Continue four miles west to Galena Creek Park. The trailhead is located at the north picnic area.

The hike: The trail follows a jeep road for about 0.5 mile then crosses Jones Creek. At the trail junction, turn right (east) to start the loop trail which then heads in a northerly direction. Climbing gradually through stands of Jeffrey pine and mountain mahogany, the trail enters Whites Canyon and then turns sharply west. Continue on the old road approximately 1.5 miles, and after entering the Mount Rose Wilderness, the trail turns right off the old road, crosses Whites Creek and heads west. At about the halfway point, the trail leaves Whites Canyon to the southeast and climbs onto an 8,000 foot ridge with excellent views. About a mile further on a spur trail leads west about 0.5 mile to a small lake, locally called Church's Pond. James E. Chruch was a professor at the University of Nevada Reno who established the first winter snow survey in the world, a system he devised on Mount Rose early in the 20th century.

The main trail continues east, switchbacking down into Jones Creek to complete the loop. At the trail junction, turn right (southeast) and follow the trail 0.5 mile to the trailhead which is back at Galena Creek Park.—*US Forest Service*

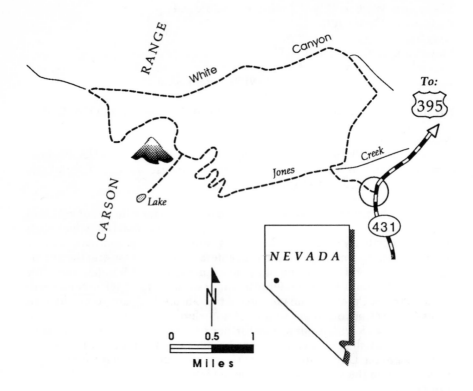

HIKE 25 *MOUNT ROSE*

General description: A round-trip day hike in the Carson Range.
General location: Approximately fifteen miles southwest of Reno.
Maps: Mt. Rose 7.5-minute USGS quad.
Difficulty: Difficult.
Length: Six miles one-way.
Elevation: 8,800 to 10,776 feet.
Special attractions: Spectacular views of the Lake Tahoe region of the Sierra Nevada.
Water: None.
Best season: Summer through fall.
For more information: Toiyabe National Forest, 1536 S. Carson St., Carson City, NV 89701; (702) 882-2766.
Permit: None.
Finding the trailhead: From Reno, drive eight miles south on US 395, then turn right (west) on NV 431. The trailhead is at the maintenance station just beyond Mount Rose Summit.

The hike: For the first 2.5 miles the walk climbs gradually on a dirt road. The trail then turns to the right off the road and crosses the headwaters basin of Galena Creek. After crossing the creek, the trail heads steeply uphill. At the halfway point the trail crosses a saddle, entering the Mount Rose Wilderness, and again turns to the right heading north toward Mount Rose. The last two miles are steep and difficult. The 360 degree view from the summit includes Lake Tahoe, the Great Basin Ranges to the east and Reno to the north. Hikers should beware of the strong winds which rake the mountain above timberline on most afternoons. Even in July it can get cold.—*US Forest Service*

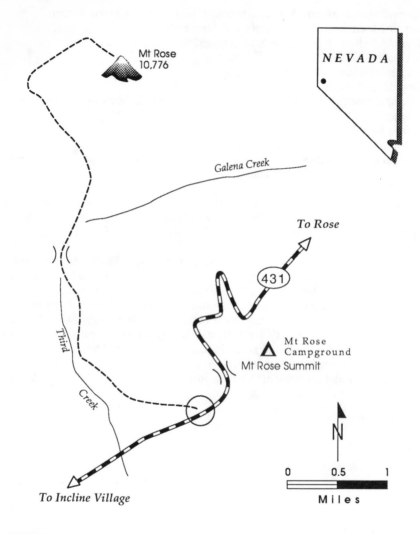

Mt Rose
10,776

NEVADA

Galena Creek

To Rose

431

Mt Rose
Campground

Mt Rose Summit

Third

Creek

To Incline Village

N

0   0.5   1

M i l e s

HIKE 26 *STAR PEAK*

General description: A round-trip day hike to the highest peak in the East Humboldt Range.

General location: Approximately fifty-six miles southwest of Winnemucca.

Maps: Star Peak 7.5-minute USGS quad.

Difficulty: Difficult.

Length: Four miles one way.

Elevation: 5,700 to 9,836 feet.

Special attractions: Expansive views.

Water: none.

Best Season: Summer through fall.

For more information: Bureau of Land Management, 705 East 4th St., Winnemucca, NV 89445; (702) 623-1500.

Permit: None.

Finding the trailhead: From Winnemucca, drive approximately fourty-six miles west on I80 and exit at the Humboldt interchange. Follow the dirt road south along the east side of the freeway approximately 4.5 miles, then turn east toward Star Peak (the highest peak) and drive three miles into Eldorado Canyon. After crossing the creek several times, the road veers left and climbs steeply out of the creek. Park here unless you have a four-wheel drive vehicle.

The hike: It is a steep hike up the road through the juniper forest but the reward is an ever-expanding view. After about 1.5 miles the road follows the ridge top east and climbs less steeply. About three miles from Eldorado Creek the road turns left (north) along the slopes of Star Peak. Leave the road and go directly up the west ridge to the summit, or continue to follow the road north until it reaches the summit ridge, then walk south up the ridge to Star Peak. There are hundred mile views in all directions, and the view of the Humboldt River Valley and Rye Patch Reservoir is especially fine.

The pygmy forest of juniper trees on the lower slopes of the Humboldt Range is almost startling to the hiker who has spent time in the ranges of northwestern Nevada. There are few trees on most of the ranges from the vicinity of Winnemucca northward and westward, the exceptions being a few junipers on the lower slopes, and a few aspens on the higher slopes. In comparison, ranges with similar elevations in eastern Nevada support varied forests. probably the lack of trees is caused by the Sierra Nevada and Cascade Mountains to the west, which intercept much of the moisture from winter storms. Very litle moisture in the form of summer thunderstorms reaches northwestern Nevada, in contrast with the active thunderstorm season further to the southeast which is closer to the source of tropical moisture.—*Bruce Grubbs*

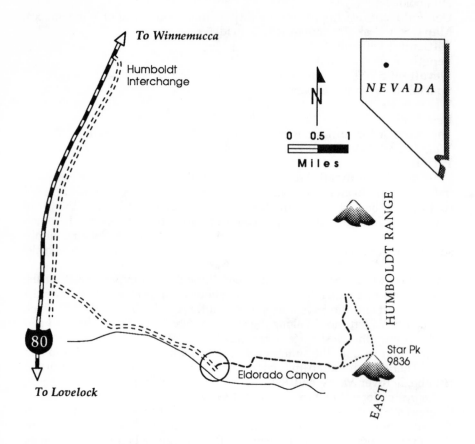

HIKE 27 *BLUE LAKES*

General description: A round-trip day hike to a glacial lake.
General location: Sixty-seven miles north of Winnemucca.
Maps: Duffer Peak 15-minute USGS quad.
Difficulty: Easy.
Length: One mile one way.
Elevation: 7,760 to 7,968 feet.
Special attractions: Glacial lakes and topographic features, pine and aspen forest.
Water: Blue Lakes; must be purified.
Best Season: Summer through fall.
For more information: Bureau of Land Management, 705 East 4th St., Winnemucca, NV 89445; (702) 623-1500.
Permit: None.
Finding the trailhead: From Winnemucca, drive thiry miles north on US 95, then forty miles west on NV 140. Turn left on the dirt road located 300 yards south of the highway maintenance station, and continue seventeen miles to Onion Valley Reservoir. A high clearance vehicle is recommended. The road to Blue Lakes trailhead goes left 1.5 miles; either park at the junction or use a four-wheel drive vehicle.

The hike: The trail winds through groves of aspen and around a terminal moraine left by the ancient glacier and proceeds to Blue Lakes, a series of clear, cold lakes set in a mountain cirque. Fed by a spring and by snow melt, the five interconnected lakes are surrounded by a mixture of willow, aspen, pine and mountain mahogany. A spur of Duffer Peak forms part of the scenic backdrop. The view from the trail yields vast panoramas that extend into California and Oregon. The lakes support a cold water fishery for trout.

Glacial moraines are distinguished from ordinary talus by the fact that they are composed of unsorted material. Talus slopes form when rocks weather and fall from cliffs. Larger rocks roll further before stopping, while small stones and pebbles tend to come to rest near the top of the slope. Likewise, rocks, sand, and silt carried by water in streams, rivers, and floods tends to be sorted by size as it is deposited, since the carrying power of moving water decreases rapidly as the speed of the water decreases. Glaciers, on the other hand, collect massive amounts of rocks and dirt as they slowly move down the mountain valleys, gouging their beds like giant bulldozers. Even more debris falls on the glacier from above, As the ice reaches lower elevations, it melts and drops its load of dirt, pebbles, rocks, and boulders in a jumbled heap. This feature is clearly visible in the Blue Lakes moraines.—*Bureau of Land Management and Bruce Grubbs*

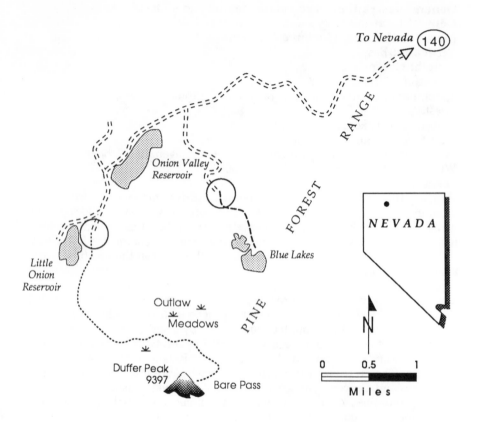

HIKE 28 *DUFFER PEAK*

General description: A cross-country round-trip day hike to the highest peak in the Pine Forest Range.

General location: Sixty-eight miles north of Winnemucca.

Maps: Duffer Peak 15-minute, Idaho Canyon 15-minute USGS quads.

Difficulty: Difficult.

Length: Three miles one way.

Elevation: 7,200 to 9,397 feet.

Special attractions: Glacial topography, pine and aspen forest.

Water: Alder Creek; should be purified.

Best Season: Summer through fall.

For more information: Bureau of Land Management, 705 East 4th St., Winnemucca, NV 89445; (702) 623-1500.

Permit: None.

Finding the trailhead: Follow the directions for Blue Lakes, but instead of taking the Blue Lakes road, continue past Onion Reservoir. At the west end of the lake, continue left over a low pass to Little Onion Reservoir. Park at the east edge of the reservoir.

The hike: The cross-country route skirts the east edge of the little lake through an aspen grove, then follows the steep drainage of Alder Creek southeast to Outlaw Meadows, a series of spacious alpine meadows. Stay on the left (north) side of this meadow past a small swampy lake, then cross the creek and head for the foot of the steep north ridge of Duffer Peak, 0.5 mile south. Pass the small but scenic Hidden Meadow and continue southeast up the steep drainage northeast of the peak. As the drainage opens out into the level expanse of Bare Pass, turn right (west) and climb the steep slopes about 0.3 mile to the rugged granite ridge which forms the summit.

From the summit, much of the forest for which the Pine Forest Range is named is visible. Whitebark and limber pine, along with quaking aspen, are rare in northwestern Nevada. This stand is considered to be a relict forest. During wetter and cooler times, when glaciers were present in a few Nevada mountins and the valleys below were covered by vast lakes, trees such as these extended over a much larger area, at lower elevations. As the climate warmed and dried, the trees, and the animals which depend on them, were forced higher into the mountins. In most of northwestern Nevada the pine forests simply disappeared, leaving only this tiny remnant.

Wildlife is relatively common because of the favorable habitat. Often seen are deer, coyote, chukar, and sage grouse, as well as waterfowl near the lakes and reservoirs. Pronghorn, bighorn sheep, bobcat, mountain lion, beaver, badger, and golden eagles are harder to spot. Also watch for birds such as the pine grosbeak and red crossbill not usually seen in this part of Nevada.—*Bruce Grubbs*

HIKE 29 *BUCKSKIN MOUNTAIN*

General description: A round-trip day hike to an 8,743 foot peak in the Santa Rosa Range.

General location: Approximately twenty-six miles northeast of Orovada.

Maps: McDermitt 15-minute USGS quad; Humboldt National Forest USFS map.

Difficulty: Moderate.

Length: two miles one way.

Elevation: 7,400 to 8,743 feet.

Special attractions: Colorful peak, with excellent views of the northern Santa Rosa Range.

Water: none.

Best Season: Summer through fall.

For more information: Humboldt National Forest, Santa Rosa Ranger District, 1200 Winnemucca Blvd. East, Winnemucca, NV 89445; (702) 623-5025.

Permit: None.

Finding the trailhead: From Orovada, drive fourteen miles north on US 95, then turn right on Forest Road 084 (signed). Follow the graveled dirt road east approximately twelve miles to Windy Gap, the pass on the crest of the Santa Rosa Range. Buckskin Mountain is the striking peak north of the road, visible from the dramatic switchbacks leading to Windy Gap. Turn north on an unmaintained road and park.

The hike: It is a moderate two-mile hike along the seldom-traveled road to the summit. Stay left at the junctions. An alternative is to follow the main ridge crest cross-country.

Seldom-traveled roads such as this one are good places to spot the tracks of one of the most elusive western animals, the mountain lion. For some reason the lions like to follow roads, at least for short distances. The large paw prints without claw marks are unmistakable, and are seen early in the day before the wind has a chance to erase the signs of their nocturnal hunting forays. Lions are extremely secretive and their tawny to grayish color blends well with the terrain, making them difficult to spot, especially during the twilight hours which are the most likely times to observe them.—*Bruce Grubbs*

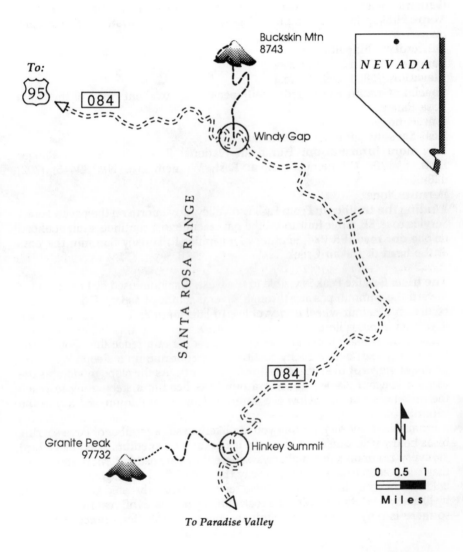

Buckskin Mtn
8743

To:
95
084

NEVADA

Windy Gap

SANTA ROSA RANGE

084

Granite Peak
97732

Hinkey Summit

N

0   0.5   1

Miles

To Paradise Valley

HIKE 30 *GRANITE PEAK*

General description: A cross-country round-trip day hike to the highest peak in the Santa Rosa Range.

General location: Approximately thirteen miles north of Paradise Valley.

Maps: Hinkey Summit 15-minute USGS quad; Humboldt National Forest USFS map.

Difficulty: Difficult.

Length: Three miles one way.

Elevation: 7,800 to 9,732 feet.

Special attractions: Rugged granite peak, with excellent views of the Santa Rosa Range.

Water: none.

Best Season: Summer through fall.

For more information: Humboldt National Forest, Santa Rosa Ranger District, 1200 Winnemucca Blvd. East, Winnemucca, NV 89445; (702) 623-5025.

Permit: None.

Finding the trailhead: From Paradise Valley, drive north on the paved Forest Service road 8B. After four miles the pavement ends; continue straight ahead on the dirt road (FR 084) another seven miles to Hinkey Summit, the pass at the head of Indian Creek.

The hike: Granite Peak is visible to the west. A seldom used dirt road climbs toward the summit, passing through several stands of aspen. This road may be driven in a four-wheel drive vehicle in late summer; earlier in the season it will be impassable due to mud and snow.

The road ends in a broad sage covered saddle at a fence line. Follow the fence left (west) over a rocky section, then continue up a steep slope with excellent views of the rugged basins to the north. As the slope moderates the summit is again visible. Contour around the head of a steep gully to reach the broad sage saddle below the summit. Now scramble up and left to the summit.

From this rocky, airy summit you are likely to see a number of large soaring birds below you. The most common is the raven, a medium sized black bird also very common along highways, where they eat road kill. More rare is the majestic golden eagle, which is nearly the size of the bald eagle but lacks the bald eagle's white head. You may also see small white-throated swifts zooming by like tiny jets, often missing the rock cliffs by inches. Swifts eat flying insects, so there is purpose to their seemingly endless aerobatics.—*Bruce Grubbs*

HIKE 31 *REBEL CREEK TRAIL*

General description: A round-trip day hike in the Santa Rosa Range.
General location: Three miles north of Orovada.
Maps: Hinkey Summit 15-minute USGS quad; Humboldt National Forest USFS map.
Difficulty: Moderate.
Length: Three miles one way.
Elevation: 5,000 to 6,800 feet.
Special attractions: Granite basin and range topography, with aspen groves.
Water: Rebel Creek is not recommended for drinking.
Best season: Summer through fall.
For more information: Humboldt National Forest, Santa Rosa Ranger District, 1200 Winnemucca Blvd. East, Winnemucca, NV 89445; (702) 623-5025.
Permit: None.
Finding the Trailhead: Drive three miles north of Orovada on US 95, and turn right at the Rebel Creek road. Continue three miles east on the dirt road, bypassing the ranch to the right (south). The road ends at the mouth of the canyon.

The hike: The foot trail is maintained and stays on the left side of the creek. After a steady climb, the trail crosses the creek and then fades out in an aspen grove well below the main crest. It is possible to continue cross-country through the sage and aspen to the crest of the Santa Rosa Range.

Cheatgrass, an introduced annual, and native grasses along with sagebrush, cover the lower drainage. Willows and cottonwoods shade the stream that supports Brook and Rainbow trout. Chukars are common game bird found in this environment. In the spring, Buttercups, Blue Bells, and Yellow Bells bloom first, followed by Lupine, Skyrockets, and Sunflowers which bloom until late July. Rattle snakes can be found in this warmer climate too.

In the higher elevation country, mahogany, aspen, serviceberry, and snowberry are the species you will see. Yellow Violets, Monkshood, and Red Columbine are found in the shade of aspen groves. Mountain and Western Blue birds, along with many raptors can be seen. Mule deer make their summer home in the high basins and draws.

The geology changes from phyllite to granite as you move to the high country. Santa Rosa Peak at 9,701 feet, is the dominant feature of the basin. The near vertical rim is crescent shaped with wind swept limber pine growing at the tree line. This peak lends its name to the nearby Santa Rosa-Paradise Peak Wilderness.—*Bruce Grubbs*

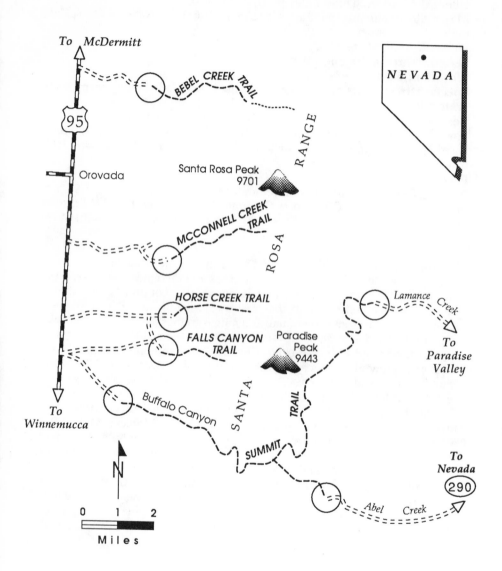

To McDermitt

BEBEL CREEK TRAIL

NEVADA

95

Orovada

Santa Rosa Peak
9701

RANGE

MCCONNELL CREEK TRAIL

ROSA

HORSE CREEK TRAIL

Lamance Creek

FALLS CANYON TRAIL

Paradise Peak
9443

To
Paradise
Valley

To
Winnemucca

Buffalo Canyon

SANTA

TRAIL

To
Nevada
290

SUMMIT

Abel Creek

N

0   1   2
Miles

HIKE 32 MCCONNELL CREEK TRAIL

General description: A short round-trip day hike in the Santa Rosa Range.
General location: Forty miles north of Winnemucca.
Maps: Hinkey Summit 15-minute USGS quad; Humboldt National Forest USFS map.
Difficulty: Moderate.
Length: Three miles one way.
Elevation: 5,000 to 6,800 feet.
Special attractions: Granite and phyllite geology, with open views of Santa Rosa Peak.
Water: McConnell Creek is not recommended for drinking
Best season: Summer through fall.
For more information: Humboldt National Forest, Santa Rosa Ranger District, 1200 Winnemucca Blvd. East, Winnemucca, NV 89445; (702) 623-5025.
Permit: None.
Finding the trailhead: Drive forty miles north of Winnemucca on US 95, and turn right at the McConnell Creek Road (signed). Continue three miles east of the highway. The trailhead is 100 yards inside the Forest Service boundary fence on the northeast side of the creek.

The hike: Minimal trail maintenance is done at the beginning of the season. The upper basin is wide with a view of Santa Rosa Peak, the striking granite peak which dominates the southern part of the range.

Phyllite outcrops and grassy hillsides greet the hiker in the lower portion of the drainage. Access to the creek is difficult due to a deeply cut channel, but Brook trout can be creeled if the fisherman is persistent. A sharp eye might catch a glimpse of the California bighorn sheep that inhabit the area to the north. A lack of trees gives an open feeling to the lower canyon.

Mid canyon brings a geologic change. Granite ridges and decomposed granite soil are the dominent features. Aspen, mountain mahogany and snowberry begin to fill the draws and slopes with willows growing in the bottoms. A stunning view of the steep and rocky west slope of Santa Rosa Peak rises above you as you enter McConnell basin. Golden eagles soar on the air currents and small lizards watch with passing interest while sunning themselves on granite rocks.—*US Forest Service*

HIKE 33 *HORSE CANYON TRAIL*

General description: A short round-trip day hike in the Santa Rosa Range.
General location: Thirty-eight miles north of Winnemucca.
Maps: Hinkey Summit 15-minute, Paradise Valley 15-minute USGS quads; Humboldt National Forest USFS map.
Difficulty: Moderate.
Length: Two miles one way.
Elevation: 5,000 to 6,500 feet.
Special attractions: Phyllite bedrock in the lower canyon gives way to granite in the upper basin.
Water: Horse Creek; not recommended for drinking.
Best season: Summer through fall.
For more information: Humboldt National Forest, Santa Rosa Ranger District, 1200 Winnemucca Blvd. East, Winnemucca, NV 89445; (702) 623-5025.
Permit: None.
Finding the trailhead: Drive thirty-eight miles north of Winnemucca on US 95, and turn right at the Horse Canyon Road (signed). Vehicles with high clearance are recommended to reach this trailhead, which is 3.5 miles east of the highway. The actual trailhead is 150 yards southeast inside the Forest Service boundary fence. From here, the trail follows the creek, becoming a cattle trail near the end.

Record snow accumulated on the Santa Rosa Mountains in 1983-1984. Then a sudden change in temperature, from freezing to 90+ degrees, in late May caused a rapid snowmelt. The ground became super saturated and the creeks swelled. Within 24 hours of the abrupt temperature change, mudslides containing massive amounts of debris and torrents of water gutted several streams. Damage caused by that hundred year flood event are still evident today. Steeply cut banks, mudslide scars, and high water debris are found in many drainages. The skeletal remains of aspen and pioneer age cottonwoods are now home to birds and small mammals.

The granite rimmed sky-line rings the basin. While sitting under a mountain mahogany in the cool breeze, you can view a wide variety of vegetation. Aspen, alders and limber pine occur on the north facing slopes which hold the snow longer. Mountain mahogany, serviceberry, snowberry and sagebrush occur in the sun dried south facing slopes. House wrens, Red-shafted flickers and Mountain chickadees call from the trees. Inconspicuous Jacob's Ladder, Penstemon, and Clarkia hide amongst the rocks.—*US Forest Service and Bruce Grubbs*

HIKE 34 *FALLS CANYON TRAIL*

General description: A short round-trip day hike in the Santa Rosa Range.
General location: Thirty-eight miles north of Winnemucca.
Maps: Hinkey Summit 15-minute, Paradise Valley 15- minute USGS quads; Humboldt National Forest USFS map.
Difficulty: Moderate.
Length: 1.5 miles one way.
Elevation: 5,000 to 6,000 feet.
Special attractions: Granite basin and range topography, with aspen and limber pine.
Water: Falls Creek is not recommended for drinking.
Best season: Summer through fall.
For more information: Humboldt National Forest, Santa Rosa Ranger District, 1200 Winnemucca Blvd. East, Winnemucca, NV 89445; (702) 623-5025.
Permit: None.
Finding the trailhead: Drive thirty-eight miles north of Winnemucca on US 95, and turn right at the Horse Canyon Road (signed). Vehicles with high clearance are recommended to reach this trailhead, which is 3.5 miles east of the highway. The actual trailhead is 100 yards northeast inside the Forest Service boundary fence.

The hike: Generally, the trail stays along the creek or just above the Forest Service boundary fence. Minimal trail maintenance is done at the beginning of the season.

Just after you enter the canyon and begin your walk up the trail, you'll come to the waterfall for which the canyon is named. It is small, but when the water is flowing wildly in the spring or is hanging in frozen needles of ice in the winter, it can be a beautiful sight. The vertical walls of phyllite to the south at the canyon entrance are awe inspiring, but quickly give way to granite features a short way up the canyon. A lone limber pine grows out of a fissure in a single granite boulder in the sagebrush basin. Robins love the choke cherries in the fall when the fruit is ripe. Elder berries can be picked and made into jelly, syrup and wine.—*US Forest Service*

Bristlecone pines are found near timberline on mountains in the southwest, and live for thousands of years. Even after death, the tough wood survives many bitter alpine winters, becoming polished by wind driven snow and burnished by the sun. Cliff Leight

HIKE 35

SANTA ROSA SUMMIT TRAIL
BUFFALO CANYON

General description: A round-trip day hike in the Santa Rosa Range.
General location: Thirty-five miles north of Winnemucca.
Maps: Five Fingers 7.5-minute, Santa Rosa Peak 7.5-minute, Hinkey Summit 7.5-minute USGS quads; Humboldt National Forest USFS map.
Difficulty: Moderate-difficult.
Length: 4.5 miles one way.
Elevation: 4,400 to 8,200 feet.
Special attractions: Solitude, wildlife, wildflowers, views typical of the Great Basin.
Water: Avoid drinking water from streams and springs because of giardia.
Best season: Summer and fall.
For more information: Humboldt National Forest, Santa Rosa Ranger District, 1200 Winnemucca Blvd. East, Winnemucca, NV 89445; (702) 623-5025.
Permit: None.
Finding the trailhead: From Winnemucca, drive thirty- five miles north on US 95, then turn right at the Buffalo Canyon road sign. Follow the dirt road two miles. The trail head begins northwest of the Forest Service boundary fence.

The hike: The first half of the trail to the crest was constructed in 1986, and passes through sagebrush, various grasses, willows and cottonwoods. The upper half is older and more primitive and passes through snowberry, serviceberry, mahogany and aspen. A steep climb to the crest completes the last 0.5 mile.

For access to the trail on the east side of the range, see Santa Rosa Summit Trail-Abel Creek and Santa Rosa Summit Trail-Lamance Creek.

The trail criss-crosses Buffalo Canyon Creek throughout it's journey to the summit at 8,000 feet. Passage in the lower part of the drainage is by a trail constructed around phyllite outcrops and narrow benches. The harsh weather conditions of mountainous country have molded the channel of Buffalo Creek. Severe thunderstorms are hazardous to both the environment and man. Be prepared for sudden changes in the weather.

Mountain lions are known to travel throughout the drainage. Mule deer can be seen browsing on the snowberry and aspen saplings in the high basins. The fall colors of the aspen and snowberry are brilliant gold, orange, yellow and red. Rabbitbrush and sagebrush are late bloomers displaying small yellow flowers.

The view to the east from the summit of Buffalo Canyon includes Paradise Valley dotted with ranches and farms, and the Snowstorm and Independence Mountains of Elko County. The Jackson and Pine Forest Mountains are to the west. A trail south along the crest affords more panoramic views.—*US Forest Service*

HIKE 36 SANTA ROSE SUMMIT TRAIL
SINGAS CREEK

General description: Day hikes and access to the southern portion of the Summit Trail.

General location: Forty-two miles northeast of Winnemucca Nevada.

Maps: Five Fingers 7.5-minute, Paradise Valley 7.5-minute. USGS quads; Humboldt National Forest USFS map.

Difficulty: Moderate to easy after you access the trail.

Length: Varied.

Elevation: 6,500 to 7,300 feet.

Special attractions: Singas Trailhead with ample parking and horse unloading facilities.

Water: Avoid drinking the water from streams and springs dut to giardia.

Best season: Summer and fall.

For more information: Humboldt National Forest, 1200 Winnemucca Blvd. East, Winnemucca, NV 89445; (702) 623-5025.

Permit: None.

Finding the trailhead: From Winnemucca, go twenty-two miles north on US 95, then turn right on NV 290 and continue 17 miles to the signed Singas Creek road. Turn left and drive five miles to the parking area. A high clearance vehicle should be used. From the parking area, follow an old road 0.5 mile up a steep climb to the trail.

The hike: The Summit Trail can be hiked south or north from Singas basin. Hidden fromview by foothills, the Singas Creek Basin is filled with aspen, peaks with vertical granite faces, and streams fed by the spring snowmelt. Views from the north or south trail summits is spectacular. Marmots chirp a sharp warning before disappearing into their rock dens. Patience may be rewarded when a curious marmot pops his head back out to gbet a look at the interloper. Downy woodpeckers nest in cavities. House wrens and Wilson's Warbler flit among the willows and aspen trees. Early morning and late evening are the mule deer's favorite time for browsing. Tall, flowering Bluebells, Larkspur, and Jewel Flower can be found. In wet meadows, the fragile Blue Flax and hardy Mountain Iris grow.—*US Forest Service*

HIKE 37 *SANTA ROSA SUMMIT TRAIL NORTH HANSON CREEK*

General description: Day hikes and access tot he Summit Trail.
General location: Fourty-four miles northeast of Winnemucca, Nevada.
Maps: Santa Rosa, Paradise Valley and Hinkey Summit SE, NV 7.5-minute USGS quads. Humboldt National Forest USFS map.
Difficulty: Easy trail, moderate difficulty to reach by vehicle.
Length: Varied.
Elevation: 6,000 to 6,400 feet.
Special attractions: It is the closest vehicle access to the Summit Trail.
Water: Avoid drinking from the streams and springs due to giardia.
Best season: Late spring to fall.
For more information: Humboldt National Forest, Santa Rosa Ranger District, 1200 Winnemucca Blvd. East, Winnemucca, NV 89445; (702) 623-5025.
Permit: None.
Finding the trailhead: From Winnemucca, go twenty-two miles north on US 95, then turn right on NV 290 and continue eighteen miles to Paradise Valley, NV. Turn right at the main intersection and drive 1.5 miles to the end of the road and turn left and continue for 0.5 mile. Turn right on the dirt road that follows the fence line that heads west. Continue up the foothill until you reach a fork in the road. Here you cross the creek and continue west up into the basin. The trail is just west of the parking area. A high clearance vehicle should be used to reach this trail.

The hike: The Summit Trail can be hiked south or north from the North Fork of Hanson. This access affords the hiker several options: 1) close vehicle parking, 2) a hike to the south where you can exit the Singas Creek Trailhead, 3) a more primitive hike to the north on a less well devined trail. This trail provides an easy to moderate hike conducive to families with small children.

Limber pines dot the granite basins high above the trail. North Hanson and Lamance drainages melt together to form one large basin. Willows, aspen, snowberry, and sagebrush dominate the landscape. Indian Paintbrush, sunflowers, and blue Forget-Me-Not greet the hiker. Red tailed hawks perch in aspen and the noisy raven is common.—*US Forest Service*

HIKE 38 *WATER CANYON*

General description: A loop day hike in the Sonoma Range.
General location: Five miles south of Winnemucca.
Maps: Winnemucca 15-minute USGS quad.
Difficulty: Difficult.
Length: Eight miles.
Elevation: 5,900 to 8,900 feet.
Special attractions: Views of the historic Humboldt River valley.
Water: none.
Best season: Summer and fall.
For more information: Bureau of Land Management, 705 East 4th St., Winnemucca, NV 89445; (702) 623-1500.
Permit: None.
Finding the trailhead: From downtown Winnemucca at the junction of business I80 and US 95, drive east 1 block, then turn right and continue about one mile to the end of the street. Turn right, and then go left at the edge of town on the dirt Water Canyon Road. Continue about five miles to the end of the road in an aspen grove.

The hike: On the left a jeep road switchbacks steeply up the slope. Either walk up the road or go directly up the slope to the right of the road. Both routes lead to the top of the ridge northeast of Water Canyon. Follow the jeep road and the ridge southeast around the head of Water Canyon to the high point about three miles north of Sonoma Peak.

It is possible to detour south to the peak; this would add about six miles round trip to the hike.

From the high point, hike cross-country along the ridge west and northwest above Water Canyon about one mile, then drop down the ridge north to reach the creek about a mile upstream of the parking area. An old road leads down the creek to the parking area.

During the walk along the high ridges, a large portion of the Humboldt River valley is visible. The Humboldt is Nevada's longest river, but in keeping with the character of the Great Basin, never reaches the sea. It rises near the town of Wells in northeastern Nevada and crosses northern Nevada to the west and then south to finally disappear in the alkaline flats of the Humboldt Sink. Although it covers only 280 airline miles, it has such a low gradient and meanders so much that the river channel is actually 1,000 miles long. The Humboldt River was a major emigrant trail during the settling of California and Oregon; the ill-fated Donner party passed this way.—*Bruce Grubbs*

HIKE 38 *WATER CANYON*

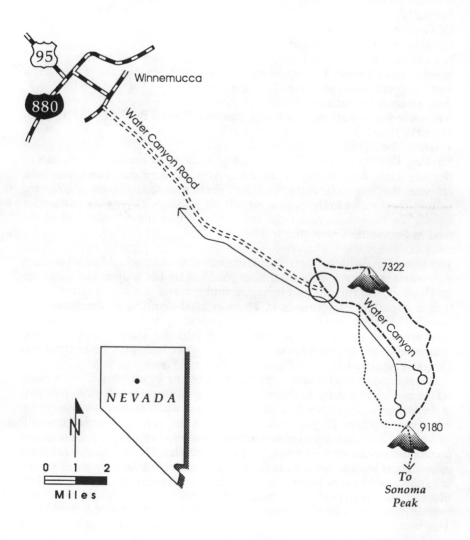

description: A two- or three-day loop hike over the major peaks of t.. ..rbidge Crest.
General location: Approximately 105 miles north of Elko.
Maps: Jarbidge 15-minute USGS quad.
Difficulty: Difficult.
Length: Twelve miles round trip.
Elevation: 6,945 to 10,839 feet.
Special attractions: Spectacular views from the highest peaks of the range.
Water: Upper Jarbidge River, Jarbidge Lake.
Best season: Summer.
For more information: Humboldt National Forest, Buhl, ID 83316; (208) 543-4219.
Permit: None.
Finding the trailhead: The Jarbidge Mountains in extreme northeastern Nevada were Nevada's first Wilderness Area. Remote and time-consuming to reach, they are well worth the effort. From Elko, go north on NV 225 for ~~seventy-three~~ 50 *fifty* miles to the signed turnoff for Jarbidge. ~~Twenty-six~~ 26 miles after leaving the pavement, turn right and continue four miles to the end of the road at Snowslide Creek (the trailhead).

The hike: The Jarbidge River Trail starts out as an old road and then becomes a new foot trail as it climbs up the canyon. The timber is open and there are excellent views. The old trail is buried under avalanche debris but the new trail is open and easy to follow. There is good camping in the vicinity of Jarbidge Lake (really a pond). Switchbacks lead up to the crest south of the lake, where a signed trail descends south into the Mary's River country. Continue up more switchbacks to the pass between Mary's River Peak and Cougar Peak. This is a good goal for a day hike.

The strenuous and difficult crest traverse begins by crossing Cougar Peak, which is relatively easy. To the north the ridge is narrow with a 250-foot cliff and bristlecone pines crowding the narrow crest. Matterhorn Peak looks steep but is easy to climb (it would be dangerous if the route was snow covered). Of course the views are excellent in all directions, and the view down the precipitous north face is dizzying. North of Matterhorn Peak the ridge becomes easier. There is some limited camping in the saddles but the only water source is snow, if available. It is possible to continue north to Jarbidge, the last high peak in the range, which has fine views north into Idaho.

Return to the trailhead by descending the steep west ridge of Jumbo Peak. This route is straightforward until about 1,000 feet above the trailhead. Here a flat terminates in steep cliffs, which can be bypassed by dropping south into Snowslide Creek. The worst of the brush can be avoided by means of deer trails.—*Bruce Grubbs*

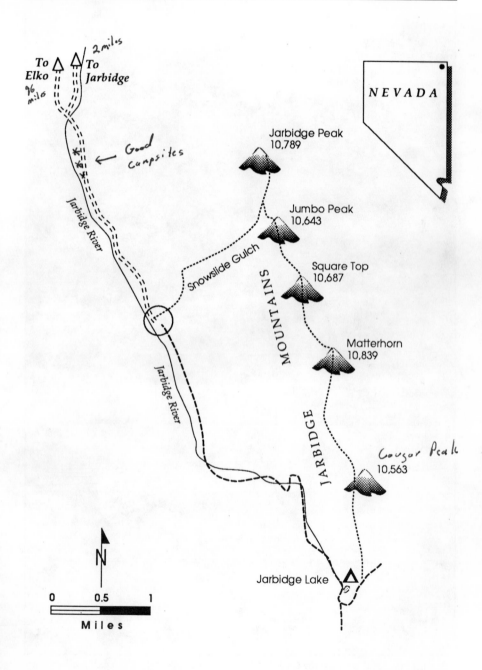

To Elko 96 miles
2 miles
To Jarbidge

Good campsites

Jarbidge River

Jarbidge River

Snowslide Gulch

NEVADA

Jarbidge Peak
10,789

Jumbo Peak
10,643

Square Top
10,687

Matterhorn
10,839

Cougar Peak
10,563

MOUNTAINS

JARBIDGE

N

0   0.5   1

Miles

Jarbidge Lake

The north trailhead for the Ruby Crest Trail is easily reached via a good paved road up spectacular Lamoille Canyon. Several Forest Service campgrounds make it easy to camp before starting the hike.

HIKE 40 *RUBY CREST TRAIL*

General description: A four-day backpack trip in the Ruby Mountains.
General location: Forty-two miles south of Elko.
Maps: Lamoille 15-minute, Franklin Lake NW 7.5- minute, Franklin Lake SW 7.5-minute, Jiggs 15-minute USGS quads.
Difficulty: Difficult.
Length: Approximately thirty-seven miles one way.
Elevation: 7,247 to 10,893 feet.
Special attractions: Classic alpine scenery, glacial valleys, cirques and mountain lakes and streams.
Water: Plentiful in lakes and streams north of Overland Lake; somewhat dryer last twelve miles to Harrison Pass.
Best season: Late summer through fall.
For more information: Humboldt National Forest, Wells, NV 89825; (702) 752-3357.
Permit: None.
Finding the trailhead: This popular and scenic trail follows the approximate crest of the Ruby Mountains from the end of the Lamoille Canyon Road about thirty-seven miles to Harrison Pass. All of the trail may be hiked one-way as a four or five day backpack trip, or either end may be hiked as day hikes of various lengths.

From Elko, drive south on NV 228 and turn left on NV 277. Just before the hamlet of Lamoille, turn right on the paved Lamoille Canyon Road (signed). Continue to the parking loop at the end of the road.

The hike: If the complete Crest Trail is hiked one way, a vehicle should be left at Harrison Pass, which is reached from Elko via NV 228. Continue past Jiggs, where the pavement ends, on the good dirt road to a junction. Turn left (east) on the signed Harrison Pass road and continue to Harrison Pass. The Ruby Crest Trail begins as a jeep road winding north along the crest.

Lamoille Canyon displays the classic U-shaped profile of a glacier-carved alpine valley. Forest Service interpretive displays along the road point out the distinctive features of the canyon. Numerous avalanche paths descend the steep walls; some years the road is blocked by a tangled mixture of trees and rock- hard snow brought down by the avalanches. The Ruby Mountains are the most alpine of Nevada ranges, with rugged granite peaks and crystal lakes.

From the trailhead, the trail climbs past Lamoille Lake over Liberty Pass, then descends past Liberty Lake to Favre Lake. After passing the turnoff to North Furlong Lake, the last of the series of glacial lakes, the trail reaches its highest point at Wines Peak. To the south of Wines Peak, the trail follows the general crest until it drops into the Overland Creek drainage and contours to Overland Lake. Above the lake the trail climbs steeply over the crest into the North Fork Smith Creek. Now the trail stays well west of the crest as it heads the west side canyons, only regaining the crest about two miles north of Harrison Pass.

The northern section of the Ruby Mountains contain more glacial lakes than any other range in Nevada. These lakes are the main reason the mountains appear so alpine. The lakes formed after the glaciers melted and runoff water

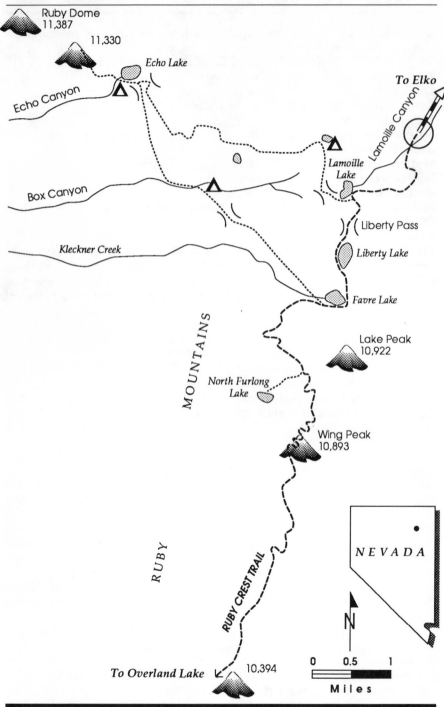

Ruby Dome
11,387

11,330

Echo Lake

Echo Canyon

Box Canyon

Kleckner Creek

MOUNTAINS

North Furlong Lake

RUBY

RUBY CREST TRAIL

To Overland Lake 10,394

To Elko

Lamoille Canyon

Lamoille Lake

Liberty Pass

Liberty Lake

Favre Lake

Lake Peak
10,922

Wing Peak
10,893

NEVADA

N

0   0.5   1
Miles

filled the depressions left behind. Glaciers tend to form depressions in their beds in two ways; by bulldozing rocks into a dam (known as a terminal moraine), or by carving out basins in the bedrock (called grinding down at the heel).—*Bruce Grubbs*

HIKE 41 *ECHO LAKE*

General description: A two- or three-day loop backpack trip in the Ruby Mountains.
General location: Forty-two miles south of Elko.
Maps: Lamoille 15-minute USGS quad.
Difficulty Difficult.
Length: Thirteen miles round-trip.
Elevation: 8,800 to 10,880 feet.
Special attractions: Scenic, lesser traveled area of the popular Ruby Mountains.
Water: Dollar, Lamoille, Echo, Favre and Liberty Lakes; Box, Kleckner and Lamoille Creeks.
Best season: Late summer through fall.
For more information: Humboldt National Forest, Wells, NV 89825; (702) 752-3357.
Permit: None.

The hike: See the Ruby Crest Trail for road directions. Follow the Ruby Crest Trail to Lamoille Lake, then leave the trail and skirt the lake on either side and climb to the saddle at the head of Box Canyon. Now contour to the right around the head of Box Canyon and generally work east to the saddle south of Echo Lake. This traverse is strenuous but the fine views and the two small unnamed hanging lakes are worth it. It is probably easier to descend into Box Canyon and climb up the side drainage to the saddle south of Echo Lake. From this saddle drop down to the lake; there are campsites in the trees near the outlet.

An optional side hike to the west, heading a cirque, leads to an 11,330 foot ridge and an excellent view of Ruby Dome, the highest peak in the range.

From Echo Lake, climb back to the saddle south of the lake, then descend the scenic hanging valley to the south into Box Canyon. There are good campsites in aspens stands in the broad valley floor. About one mile east of the point where Box Creek is first reached, climb south over a saddle then contour east into the head of Kleckner Creek. Some sections of the traverse are rough.

Both Kleckner and Box Canyons are very scenic, with grassy north slopes, pine-forested south slopes and aspen glades in the canyon floors. At the west end of Favre Lake, rejoin the Ruby Crest Trail.

Follow the trail east and north around Favre Lake and up to Liberty Lake, over Liberty Pass and past Lamoille Lake to the trailhead.

Glacial features such as horn shaped peaks, cirques, hanging valleys, and U-shaped valleys dominate the scenery on this rugged loop. Cirques are the birthplace of glaciers, which start to form when more snow falls than melts each year. After many layers of snow are deposited, the weight compresses

Especially in the late summer and fall, Nevada's mountain weather can change rapidly. Here, the clouds are clearing after an October storm in the Ruby Mountains.

the lower layers into ice, which begins to flow slowly downhill. At the heads of the valleys, the ice eats away at all three slopes. After the glacier melts, the classic bowl-shaped valley head is exposed, often containing one or more deep lakes. The mountain summits, their flanks worn away by the ice in the valleys, present sheer faces and knife edge ridges. As the ice progresses down the valleys, it carves away at the sides, converting the V-shaped valley created by water to a U-shape. Side glaciers contribute ice to the main glacier just as creeks contribute water to a river. The main glacier lowers its bed much faster than its tributaries, so that when the ice melts, hanging valleys are formed with floors much higher than the main valley. The ice also leaves behind such telltale signs as moraines and polished rock slabs with scratches showing the directions the ice moved.—*Bruce Grubbs*

HIKE 42 *OVERLAND LAKE LOOP*

General description: A loop day hike or two-day backpack in the Ruby Mountains.
General location: Approximately sixty miles southeast of Elko.
Maps: Franklin Lake NW 7.5-minute USGS quad.
Difficulty Difficult.
Length: Fourteen miles round-trip.
Elevation: 6,120 to 10,160 feet.
Special attractions: Alpine lake and scenery, superb views of the Ruby Valley.
Water: Mayhew Creek and Overland Lake.
Best season: Late summer through fall.
For more information: Humboldt National Forest, Wells, NV 89825; (702) 752-3357.
Permit: None.
Finding the trailhead: Access to the spectacular east side of the Ruby Mountains is difficult due to the private land along the foothills. Overland Lake is an exception, being reachable by Forest Service trail. From Elko, drive east on I80 twenty miles, then right (southeast) on NV 229 over Secret Pass. The paved road continues south along the east side of the range for several miles, then abruptly turns northeast at a junction. Continue south on the dirt Ruby Valley road approximately seventeen miles and park at the jeep trail shown on the topo just north of Mayhew Creek, about a mile north of Rock House.

The hike: Do not follow the jeep trail. The Overland Lake Trail follows the fence, crosses the small drainage, and again follows the fence. This section is confused by numerous cattle trails. At the section corner where the topo shows the elevation 6278, another trail comes through a gate from the left (south). Above this point the trail is more distinct. Stay on the trail approximately one mile; when the trail turns right and starts away from the creek and up the slope, drop down and cross the nameless north fork of Mayhew Creek as well as the main creek. These crossings are brushy but the walking is better on the far side. Follow the ridge just south of the main creek all the way to the crest. Hike north along the ridge less than 0.2 mile to join the Ruby Crest Trail.

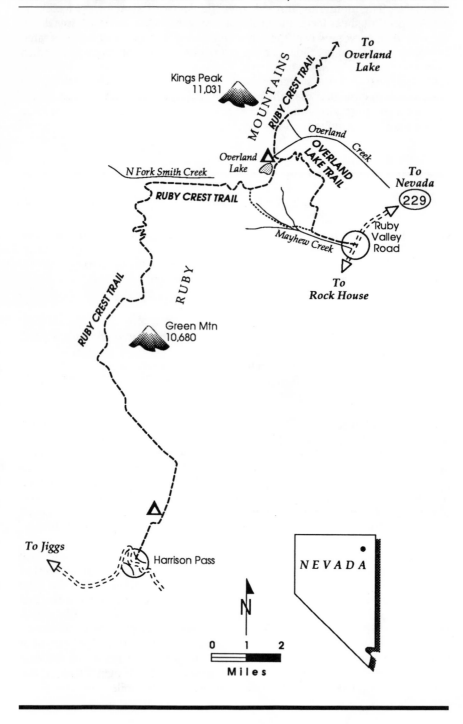

To
Overland
Lake

Kings Peak
11,031

MOUNTAINS

RUBY CREST TRAIL

Overland Creek

OVERLAND
LAKE TRAIL

Overland
Lake

To
Nevada
(229)

N Fork Smith Creek

RUBY CREST TRAIL

Mayhew Creek

Ruby
Valley
Road

To
Rock House

RUBY

RUBY CREST TRAIL

Green Mtn
10,680

To Jiggs

Harrison Pass

NEVADA

N

0   1   2

Miles

The trail climbs about 300 feet to a saddle, then descends steeply to Overland Lake, which is perched in a scenic glacial cirque. Follow the trail around the east side of the lake, and then down the steep forested slopes below the lake about 0.3 mile to the junction with the Overland Lake Trail. Turn right (east) and continue as the trail crosses the south slopes of Overland Canyon then works its way south into the Mayhew Creek drainage. A one mile descent leads to Mayhew Creek and the point where the trail was left.—*Bruce Grubb*

HIKE 43 *HENDRYS CREEK*

General description: An overnight backpack or long round-trip day hike in the Snake Range.
General location: Eighty miles east of Ely.
Maps: Mt Moriah 7.5-minute, Old Mans Canyon 7.5- minute, The Cove 7.5-minute USGS quads; Humboldt National Forest USFS map.
Difficulty Difficult.
Length: Seven miles one way.
Elevation: 6,000 to 9,100 feet.
Special attractions: Scenic canyon, large aspen groves, access to "The Table" and Mt. Moriah.
Water: Hendry's Creek.
Best season: Summer through fall.
For more information: Humboldt National Forest, 150 E. 8th Ave., Ely, NV 89301; (702) 289-3031.
Permit: None.
Finding the trailhead: From Ely, go east fifty-eight miles on US 6-50 to the junction of US 6-50 and NV 487 (the highway to Baker and Great Basin National Park). The following mileages are from the Y Cafe at the junction. Continue 0.2 miles east on US 6-50, then turn left (north) on an unsigned gravel road for 10.7 miles to a well graded road coming from the right. Less than 0.1 mile before the junction, a rock cairn signed "Hatch Rock" marks a graded dirt road going left (northwest). Take this road 2.9 miles through a gate and past a "Hatch Rock Co." sign. Continue and watch for Forest Service "Trailhead" signs. Follow these signs ignoring any side roads. A sign marks the National Forest boundary; park 0.1 mile further at an obvious parking area, 14.7 miles from the Y Cafe. A sign points out the Hendrys Creek Trail.

The hike: The first two to three miles of trail follows an old road which is severely washed out but has received Forest Service trail maintenance. The Mount Moriah Wilderness Area, established in 1989, is reached 1.5 miles from the trail head. At 5.5 miles is a signed junction with the Silver Creek Trail. Stay on the main trail, which becomes obscure in a few places. If in doubt, stay in the main drainage. Here the trail goes through continuous aspen groves. One and a half miles from the Silver Creek Trail junction the trail comes to a meadow bordered on three sides with aspen and good camping. To the west are views of the south side of Mt. Moriah, and there are spectacular views

HIKE 43 *HENDRYS CREEK*

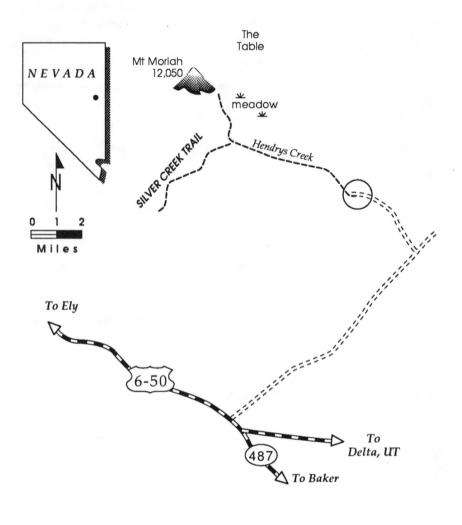

down Hendrys Creek canyon. Beyond this meadow, Hendrys Creek forks several times and the trail becomes consistently difficult to follow.

This point can be used as a base for hikes to "The Table", an 11,000 foot plateau, or to Mt. Moriah (12,050 feet).—*Ron Kezar*

A number of ice-age glacers carved the classic alpine terrain of the Snake Range, leaving behind such features as the imposing Wheeler Cirque shown here, as well as numerous small alpine lakes. All of the ice is gone now, except for the Wheeler Icefield, which is the only permanent ice between the Sierra Nevada of California and the Wasatch Range of Utah. Stewart Aitchison

HIKE 44 *LEHMAN CREEK TRAIL*

General description: A round-trip day hike in the Snake Range.
General location: Nine miles west of Baker.
Maps: Windy Peak 7.5-minute USGS quad.
Difficulty Difficult.
Length: Four miles one way.
Elevation: 7,800 to 9,950 feet.
Special attractions: Hiker's alternative to the Scenic Drive.
Water: None.
Best season: Summer.
For more information: Great Basin National Park, Baker, NV 89311; (702) 234-7331.
Permit: None.

The hike: This trail connects the Upper Lehman Creek Campground with the Wheeler Peak Campground . Both these campgrounds are located along the Wheeler Peak Scenic Drive, and this trail provides an alternative to the road.

Lehman Creek and Lehman Caves are named after Absalom Lehman, a settler who arrived in the area in 1869. He established a fruit orchard adjacent to what is now the Visitor Center parking lot and began supplying apricots, pears, peaches, and apples to the booming mining towns. Today only eight trees survive, and they are being managed by the Park to preserve the unique genetic resource.

Great Basin National Park includes the former Lehman Caves National Monument, protecting one of the most decorated limestone solution caves in the west. Guided tours are offered daily along a two-thirds mile long trail through the cave.—*National Park Service and Bruce Grubbs*

HIKE 45 *WHEELER PEAK*

General location: Seventeen miles west of Baker, Nevada.
Maps: Wheeler Peak 7.5-minute, Windy Peak 7.5-minute USGS, NPS brochure.
Difficulty Difficult.
Length: Four miles.
Elevation: 10,160 to 13,063 feet.
Special attractions: Outstanding alpine views.
Water: None.
Best season: Summer.
For more information: Great Basin National Park, Baker, NV 89311; (702) 234-7331.
Permit: None.
Finding the trailhead: From Baker, drive west five miles on the Great Basin National Park entrance road (NV 488), then turn right (north) on the Wheeler Peak Scenic Drive. The road ends at the Wheeler Park Campground; backtrack and park 0.5 mile before the end of the road at the Wheeler Summit Trailhead to avoid the limited parking at the campground.

The hike: The trail travels west through stands of aspen along the southern slopes of Bald Mountain. Openings in the aspen stands provide outstanding views of the route up Wheeler Peak. After one mile of easy hiking you will intersect with the trail coming from Wheeler Peak Campground. There is another intersection about 100 yards further to the west. This is the trail to the summit of Wheeler Peak.

The trail climbs through a wide meadow before a long switchback climbs to the main crest; please do not cut the switchback as the plants are very fragile. Continue along the traverse until you gain the ridgeline at an elevation of almost 11,000 feet. Stunted and gnarled trees of limber pine and Englemann spruce indicate treeline. Views are commanding to the east and west. The clear waters of Stella Lake are visible 1,000 feet below to the east.

Climb south up the wide ridgeline over shifty quartzite scree and rocks. At the 12,000 foot level, the trail passes rock piles used for windbreaks. Hardy alpine plants such as phlox and sky pilot shelter here, finding a niche in the harsh environment. The final 1,000-foot climb to the summit is steep. Stay on the trail unless it is snow covered. If the trail is covered with snow chose your route carefully. Do not proceed if a safe route cannot be located. The snow slopes can be icy and very slippery and are located above high cliffs.

The summit is a long ridgeline with the highest point locatd in the center, overlooking the valleys 7,000 feet below.

Trees and plants growing at the treeline must adapt to the arctic environment of strong wind, severe cold, and abrasive wind blown snow. The trees tend to form dense low mats for protection from the cold, in areas where snow drifts form. The snow banks provide insulation and protection from the strong abrading effect of wind driven snow crystals. The parts of the trees that rise above the drift level often lose the branches on the windward side, forming characteristic "flag" trees. Other plants such as phlox grow in small dense mats in sheltered areas among the rocks.—*National Park Service and Bruce Grubbs*

From 13,063 foot Wheeler Peak in the Snake Range, the desert basins lie more than 7,000 feet below.

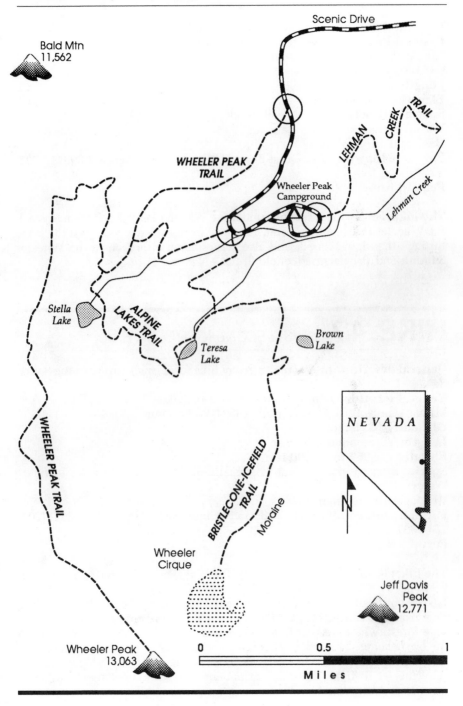

Scenic Drive

Bald Mtn
11,562

WHEELER PEAK
TRAIL

LEHMAN CREEK TRAIL

Wheeler Peak
Campground

Lehman Creek

Stella
Lake

ALPINE LAKES TRAIL

Teresa
Lake

Brown
Lake

NEVADA

N

WHEELER PEAK TRAIL

BRISTLECONE-ICEFIELD TRAIL

Moraine

Wheeler
Cirque

Jeff Davis
Peak
12,771

Wheeler Peak
13,063

0   0.5   1

Miles

HIKE 46 *ALPINE LAKES LOOP TRAIL*

General description: A loop hike past alpine lakes in the Snake Range.
General location: Seventeen miles west of Baker.
Maps: Windy Peak 7.5-minute USGS, NPS brochure.
Difficulty Easy.
Length: Three miles.
Elevation: 10,000 feet.
Special attractions: Easy trail, moderate grades, alpine lakes.
Water: Stella and Teresa Lakes.
Best season: Summer.
For more information: Great Basin National Park, Baker, NV 89311; (702) 234-7331.
Permit: None.

The hike: Follow the directions under the Wheeler Peak description to reach the Wheeler Peak Campground. This trail forms an easy loop past the lakes through the alpine forest, and also serves as an approach to the Wheeler Summit and Bristlecone/Icefield Trails.—*National Park Service*

HIKE 47 *BRISTLECONE/ICEFIELD TRAIL*

General description: A round-trip day hike to a glacial cirque in the Snake Range.
General location: Seventeen miles west of Baker.
Maps: Windy Peak 7.5-minute USGS, NPS brochure.
Difficulty Moderate.
Length: Three miles one-way.
Elevation: 9,960 to 11,200 feet.
Special attractions: Ancient bristlecone pines and the Wheeler Icefield.
Water: None.
Best season: Summer.
For more information: Great Basin National Park, Baker, NV 89311; (702) 234-7331.
Permit: None.

The hike: Follow the directions under the Wheeler Peak description to reach the Wheeler Peak Campground. Then follow the south branch of the Alpine Lakes Loop Trail and turn east onto the Bristlecone/Icefield Trail, about one mile from the campground. After another mile, one enters the bristlecone pine forest, where a short interpretive trail provides more information on the bristlecones. The trail continues to spectacular Wheeler Cirque, carved into the north face of Wheeler Peak by an ice age glacier. The trail ends at the Wheeler Icefield, the only permanent body of ice between the Sierra Nevada and the Wasatch Range.

Great Basin National Park is Nevada's first National Park and is intended to protect a typical cross section of Great Basin topography and wildlife. There are many hiking opportunities within the Park. Stewart Aitchison

The bristlecone pine is a gnarled, tough tree of the timberline regions of the Southwest, and is easily recognized by its short, stiff needles growing five to a bundle; the branches resemble foxtails. Bristlecones are the oldest living things on earth—a tree in the White Mountains just over the state line in California has been tree ring dated at 4,600 years.

Tree ring dating is done without damaging the trees, by driving a slender cylinder into the heart of the tree. The cylinder is removed and the wood core extracted. Bands along the core are sections of the tree rings, and each ring represents a period of growth. Since bristlecones have one short period of growth each year, the rings may be counted and correlated with other tree ring data to accurately determine the tree's age, as well as indicate climate changes affecting the tree's growth rate.—*National park Service and Bruce Grubbs*

HIKE 48 *BAKER CREEK TRAIL*

General description: A round-trip day hike to a glacial lake in the Snake Range.

General location: Nine miles west of Baker.

Maps: Wheeler Peak 7.5-minute, Kious Spring 7.5- minute USGS, NPS brochure.

Difficulty Difficult.

Length: Five miles.

Elevation: 7,930 to 10,630 feet.

Special attractions: Glacial lake, excellent views of high peaks.

Water: Seasonal.

Best season: Summer.

For more information: Great Basin National Park, Baker, NV 89311; (702) 234-7331.

Permit: None.

Finding the trailhead: From NV 487 approximately five miles west of Baker, turn south on the Baker Creek road and continue to the end, 0.6 mile above the Baker Creek Campground.

The hike: The trail follows Baker Creek approximately five miles to Baker Lake, located in the deep, glacially carved cirque south of Baker Peak. The trail leads through typical plant communities and provides excellent views of the peaks.—*National Park Service*

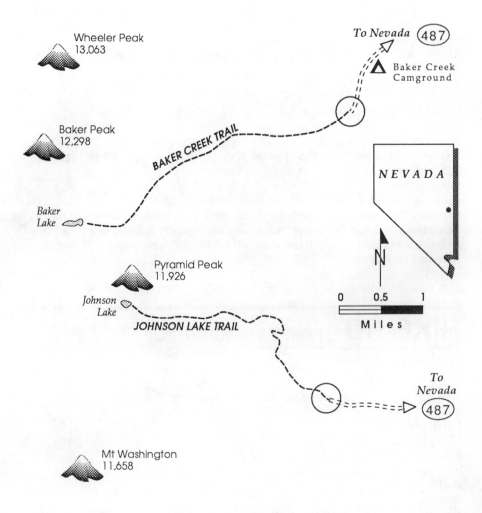

Wheeler Peak
13,063

To Nevada (487)

△ Baker Creek
Camground

Baker Peak
12,298

BAKER CREEK TRAIL

Baker
Lake

NEVADA

N

0   0.5   1

Miles

Pyramid Peak
11,926

*Johnson
Lake*

JOHNSON LAKE TRAIL

*To
Nevada*
(487)

Mt Washington
11,658

HIKE 49 *Johnson Lake Trail*

General description: A round-trip day hike to an alpine lake in the Snake Range.

General location: Eighteen miles southwest of Baker.

Maps: Wheeler Peak 7.5-minute; Kious Spring 7.5 USGS quads.

Difficulty Difficult.

Length: Five miles one way.

Elevation: 8,200 to 10,600 feet.

Special attractions: Alpine lake in a glacial cirque.

Water: Snake Creek, Johnson Lake.

Best season: Summer through fall.

For more information: Great Basin National Park, Baker, NV 89311; (702) 234-7331.

Permit: None.

Finding the trailhead: From Baker, drive south on NV 487 approximately six miles, and turn right (west) on the Snake Creek road. Follow this road to its end, approximately twelve miles. The trail mostly follows old jeep trails and is not marked or maintained, so skill with the topo maps is required.— *National Park Service*

HIKE 50 *LEXINGTON ARCH TRAIL*

General description: A round-trip day hike to a natural arch in the Snake Range.

General location: Twenty-four miles southwest of Baker.

Maps: Arch Canyon 7.5-minute USGS, NPS brochure.

Difficulty Moderate.

Length: One mile one way.

Elevation: 7,440 to 8,440 feet.

Special attractions: Natural arch, remote section of the Park.

Water: None.

Best season: Summer.

For more information: Great Basin National Park, Baker, NV 89311; (702) 234-7331.

Permit: None.

Finding the trailhead: From Baker, drive southeast on NV 487 10.7 miles (the road becomes UT 21), then turn right on the first dirt road past Pruess Lake. Proceed west twelve miles, following the signs for Lexington Arch. This road is unmaintained and a high-clearance vehicle is recommended. Please leave all gates as you find them, to help keep livestock on its proper range.

The hike: The trailhead is signed but the trail is steep, rocky, and sometimes obscure. Once you reach the base of the arch, the trail swings around the left base of the arch. From here you can climb into the arch's opening.

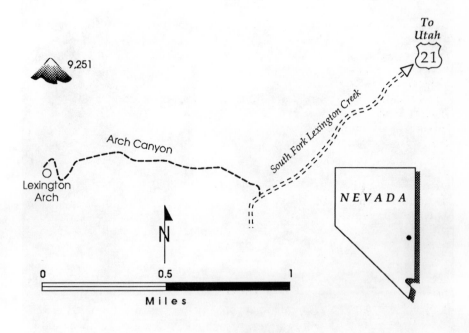

Rising high above the floor of Lexington Canyon, this imposing natural arch was created by the forces of weather working slowly over a span of centuries. Lexington Arch is unusual in one important respect: it is carved from limestone. Most of the natural arches of the western United States are composed of sandstone. The fact that Lexington Arch is made of limestone leads to speculation that it was once a passage in a cave system. Flowstone, a smooth, glossy deposit that forms in caves has been found at the base of the opening, lending support to this theory. It is even possible that Lexington "Arch" is actually a natural bridge. The distinction: an arch is formed by the forces of weathering, such as ice, wind, and chemical breakdown of the rock . A natural bridge, by contrast, is formed by the flowing waters of a stream. It is possible that long ago, when Lexington Canyon was less deep, the waters of Lexington Creek flowed through a cave in the wall of the canyon, in the process enlarging the tunnel that later became Lexington Arch. If this happened then the "Arch" is truly a bridge.—*National Park Service*

Nevada has over five million acres of land classified as Wilderness Study Areas. Stewart Aitchison

AFTERWORD

Nevada's Wilderness Challenge

Nevada is the most mountainous state, the driest state, and the fastest growing state in the country. Until recently, its vast wild places were relatively unknown except to a few hardy souls (including John Muir) who discovered the expanses of high desert cut by over 100 north-south trending mountain ranges now traversed by growing numbers of hikers.

On December 5, 1989, President Bush signed the Nevada Wilderness Bill, incorporating 732,000 acres of Forest Service land into the National Wilderness System. The bill was the result of a twenty- five year campaign to achieve formal wilderness designation for some magnificent wildlands. Prior to this date only the 64,000 acre Jarbidge Wilderness, grandfathered in under the 1964 Wilderness Act, represented the sum total of Nevada wilderness. Conservationists pushed for a 1.4 million acre bill and will work in the future to include most of the 700,000 acres omitted in the legislation.

But a far bigger battle is in store. Nevada, the largest BLM state except for Alaska, has over five million acres of lands classified as Wilderness Study Areas. Approximately two million acres are recommended by the BLM itself. These areas range from the spectacular forested peak of 10,990 foot Mt. Grafton in Eastern Nevada to the enormous expanse of the Black Rock Desert in Northwest Nevada to the red rock country of the Muddy and Mormon mountains in Southern Nevada. It will take a strong and united effort on the part of conservationists and hikers to achieve wilderness status for these remote lands. In addition, both Sheldon Antelope Range and the Desert Wildlife Range have hundreds of thousands of acres of de facto wilderness.

The potential for a real wilderness base in Nevada is unlimited. However, it will take hard work and probably many years to achieve. In the meantime we need wilderness enthusiasts to get out and enjoy what Nevada has to offer and spread the word to others.—*Marjorie Sill*

A HIKER'S BASIC CHECKLIST

Too many of us hike into the backcountry and discover we've forgotten something. No one will always take everything in the following list, but checking it before leaving home will help ensure that some essential item has not been forgotten.

- ☐ day pack or backpack
- ☐ sleeping bag
- ☐ foam pad or air mattress
- ☐ ground sheet, plastic or nylon
- ☐ dependable tent
- ☐ sturdy footwear
- ☐ lightweight camp shoes
- ☐ sunglasses
- ☐ maps and compass
- ☐ matches in waterproof container
- ☐ toilet paper
- ☐ pocket knife
- ☐ sunburn cream
- ☐ good insect repellent
- ☐ lip balm
- ☐ flashlight with new batteries
- ☐ candle(s)
- ☐ first aid kit
- ☐ survival kit
- ☐ small garden trowel or shovel
- ☐ fifty feet of nylon cord
- ☐ water filter or purification tablets
- ☐ one-quart water container
- ☐ one-gallon water container for camp use (collapsible)
- ☐ plastic bags (for trash)
- ☐ soap
- ☐ towel
- ☐ toothbrush
- ☐ cooking pots
- ☐ spoon and fork
- ☐ backpack stove and extra fuel
- ☐ aluminum foil (as windscreen for backpack stove or candle holder)
- ☐ pot scrubber
- ☐ enough food, plus a little extra
- ☐ fishing license
- ☐ fishing rod, reel, flies, lures, etc.
- ☐ camera and film
- ☐ binoculars
- ☐ waterproof covering for pack
- ☐ watch
- ☐ dependable rain parka
- ☐ rain pants
- ☐ wind garment
- ☐ thermal underwear (polypropylene is best)
- ☐ shorts and/or long pants
- ☐ wool cap or balaclava
- ☐ wool shirt and/or sweater
- ☐ jacket or parka (fiberpile is excellent)
- ☐ extra socks
- ☐ underwear
- ☐ lightweight shirts
- ☐ bandanas
- ☐ mittens or gloves
- ☐ belt
- ☐ sewing kit
- ☐ hat

Forgetting a vital piece of camping gear can be prevented by following the hiker's checklist.

RESOURCES

Bureau of Land Management

Battle Mountain District Office, 825 N. 2nd, P.O. Box 194, Battle Mountain, NV 89820; (702) 631-5181

Carson City District Office, 1535 Hot Springs Rd., Suite 300, Carson City, NV 89701; (702) 882-1631

Elko District Office, 3900 E. Idaho St., P.O. Box 831, Elko, NV 89801; (702) 738-4071

Ely District Office, Pioche Hwy., Star Route 5, Box 1, Ely, NV 89301; (702) 289-4865

Las Vegas District Office, 4765 Vegas Dr., P.O. Box 5408, Las Vegas, NV 89108; (702) 646-8800

Nevada State Office, 850 Harvard Way, P.O. Box 12000, Reno, NV 89520; (702) 784-5748

Stateline Resource Area, P.O. Box 26569, Las Vegas, NV 89126; (702) 363-1921

Susanville District Office, P.O. Box 1090, 705 Hall St., Susanville, CA, 96130; (916) 257-5385

Winnemucca District Office, 705 E. 4th St., Winnemucca, NV 89445; (702) 623-1500

Conservation Organizations and Hiking Clubs

Friends of Nevada Wilderness, P.O. Box 19777, Las Vegas, NV 89132

Nevada Outdoor Recreation Association, P.O. Box 1245, Carson City, NV 89702

Sierra Club, 5428 College Ave, Oakland, CA, 94618; (415) 654-7847

Sierra Club, Toiyabe Chapter, P.O. Box 8096, Reno, NV 89507

National Park Service

Great Basin National Park, Baker, NV 89311; (702) 234-7331

Lake Mead National Recreation Area, 601 Nevada Highway, Boulder City, NV 89005; (702) 293-8907

Nevada Division of Parks

Nevada Division of Parks, 1060 Mallory Way, Carson City, NV 89701; (702) 885-4379

Nevada Division of Parks, 201 S. Fall, Carson City, NV 89701; (702) 885-4384

Nevada Division of Parks, 4747 Vegas Dr., Las Vegas, NV 89108; (702) 486-5126

Tribal Governments

Pyramid Lake Piute Tribe, P.O Box 256, Nixon, NV 89424; (702) 574-0140

United States Fish and Wildlife Service

Charles Sheldon National Wildlife Refuge, P.O. Box 111, Lakeview, OR, 97630; (503) 947-3315

Desert National Wildlife Refuge, 1500 N. Decatur Blvd., Las Vegas, NV 89108; (702) 646-3401

Ruby Lake National Wildlife Refuge, Ruby Valley, NV 89833; (702) 779-2237

US Fish and Wildlife Service, 4600 Kietzke Ln., Bldg C Room 120, Reno, NV 89502; (702) 784-5227

United States Forest Service

Ely Ranger District, Humboldt National Forest, 350 E. 8th, Ely, NV 89301; (702) 289-3031

Jarbidge Ranger District, Humboldt National Forest, Buhl, ID 83316; (208) 543-4219.

Mountain City Ranger District, Humboldt National Forest, Mountain City, NV 89831; (702) 763-6691

Santa Rosa Ranger District, Humboldt National Forest, 1200 Winnemucca Blvd. E., Winnemucca, NV 89445; (702) 623-5025

Wells Ranger District, Humboldt National Forest, Wells, NV 89825; (702) 752-3357.

Supervisors Office, Humboldt National Forest, 976 Mountain City Hwy., Elko, NV 89801; (702) 738-5171

Austin Ranger District, Toiyabe National Forest, Main and 5th, Austin, NV 89310; (702) 964-2671

Bridgeport Ranger District, Toiyabe National Forest, Bridgeport, CA, 93517; (714) 932-7070

Carson Ranger District, Toiyabe National Forest, 1536 S. Carson, Carson City, NV 89701; (702) 882-2766

Las Vegas Ranger District, Toiyabe National Forest, 550 E. Charleston Blvd., Las Vegas, NV 89104; (702) 388-6255

Supervisors Office, Toiyabe National Forest, 1200 Franklin Way, Sparks, NV 89431; (702) 331-6444

Tonopah Ranger District, Toiyabe National Forest, P.O. Box 989, Tonopah, NV 89049; (702) 482-6286

Intermountain Regional Office, US Forest Service, 324 - 25th St., Ogden, UT, 84401; (801) 625-5182

FURTHER READING

Cline, Gloria Griffen. *Exploring the Great Basin.* University of Nevada Press: Reno, Nevada, 1963.

Elliott, Russel R. *History of Nevada.* University of Nebraska Press: Lincoln, Nebraska, 1987.

Hart, John. *Hiking the Great Basin.* Sierra Club, San Francisco, California, 1981.

Houghton, Samuel G. *A Trace of Desert Waters: The Great Basin Story.* Howe Brothers, Salt Lake City, Utah, 1986.

Larson, Peggy. *The Sierra Club Naturalist's Guide to the Deserts of the Southwest.* Sierra Club Books, San Francisco. California, 1977.

Perry, John and Jane Greverus. *Guide to the Natural Areas of New Mexico, Arizona, and Nevada.* Sierra Club Books, San Francisco, California, 1985.

Redfern, Ron. *The Making of a Continent.* Times Books: New York, New York, 1983.

Wilkerson, James. *Medicine for Mountaineering.* The Mountaineers: Seattle, Washington, 1985.

FINDING MAPS

Nevada Forest Service maps may be obtained from the Intermountain Regional Office at 324 - 25th St., Ogden, UT 84401; (801) 625- 5182, as well as from most ranger stations. Local hiking shops often stock Forest Service maps.

Bureau of Land Management maps may be obtained from the District offices listed under Resources, and from the U.S. Geological Survey (see below).

Topographic maps may be obtained from the U.S. Geological Survey, Distribution Branch, Box 25286, Denver Federal Center, Denver, CO 80225. Request the free Nevada indexes and order forms for 7.5 and 15-minute topographic maps, as well as 1:125,000 topographic and planimetric maps. The 1:125,000 index covers Bureau of Land Management maps. Many hiking shops and some engineering supply shops also stock 7.5 and 15-minute topographic maps. Note that while many of the hikes refer to 15-minute maps, these older maps are being rapidly replaced by the newer and more detailed 7.5- minute maps. Before ordering or buying a 15-minute map, check if a 7.5-minute is available.

ABOUT THE AUTHOR

Bruce Grubbs has been actively backpacking and hiking in the Southwest for more than twenty years. He has written one previous book, *The Hiker's Guide to Arizona*, with Stewart Aitchison. He lives in Flagstaff, Arizona and is a commercial pilot for a commuter airline.